HOUSE
COMFORTABLE

HOUSE COMFORTABLE

The Art & Science of Comfortable Living

Katharine Kaye McMillan

Patricia Hart McMillan

A Perigee Book

A Perigee Book
Published by The Berkley Publishing Group
200 Madison Avenue
New York, NY 10016

Copyright © 1996 by Katharine Kaye McMillan and
Patricia Hart McMillan
Book design by Rhea Braunstein
Interior illustrations copyright © 1996 by Suellen Crowley
Cover design by Joe Lanni
Cover photo courtesy of Henredon Furniture
Photo of the authors by PING DAI

First edition: September 1996

Published simultaneously in Canada.

The Putnam Berkley World Wide Web site address is
http://www.berkley.com

Library of Congress Cataloging-in-Publication Data

McMillan, Katharine Kaye.
    House comfortable : the art and science of comfortable living /
  Katharine Kaye McMillan and Patricia Hart McMillan.—1st ed.
        p.   cm.
    ISBN 0-399-52234-4
      1. Interior decoration—United States.   2. Interior decoration—
  Human factors—United States.   3. Human comfort—United
  States.   4. Architectural design—United States.   5. Life style—
  United States.   I. McMillan, Patricia Hart.   II. Title.
  NK2003.M35   1996   96-2577
  747—dc20   CIP

Printed in the United States of America

10   9   8   7   6   5   4   3   2   1

DEDICATED TO

Tessie Hart Malone,
whose house is always
home for our hearts,

and

our intrepid editors, Irene Prokop and Suzanne Bober

Contents

Comfortable is a pair of jeans, a cotton T-shirt, a pullover sweater, a cool breeze on a sweltering day, a chair that cradles a world-weary body, a quilt-covered bed, a total feeling of well-being. Your home should feel just as good and roomy and easy as putting on your favorite pair of time-worn jeans. Home should be easy, workable, and convenient, as well as adaptable, flexible, and *comfortable*.

We demand comfort in our clothing, furnishings, surroundings, and in the rituals and rhythms of daily life. Common sense has brought the dictum of comfort into play in the arena of interior design. A modern necessity, comfort goes beyond beauty, style, trend, or any decorating budget. It encompasses a wealth of options and opinions, moods and meanings, similarities and differences. Comfort has come into its own as style and lifestyle.

House Comfortable is a new and distinctly different approach to design. Rooms that must be designed for maximum convenience are the kitchen and bath, followed in importance by the bedroom, dining room, living room, and sitting room. *House Comfortable* is a uniquely American approach to design, a logical extension of the same design criteria that has made blue jeans a standard of comfort and style.

Up until now, the home itself and all *equipment* for the home was designed for the mythical model man who, at six feet tall and 190 pounds, was perpetually thirty-something years old and in the best of health. He never slouched around the house, raised children, or had his aging parents over for a stay, nor did he succumb to illness or disabilities. Perhaps you married this paragon or you are him, only older and better, but you have noticed that your house and its equipment for living are inconvenient, unworkable, or even downright hazardous to your health.

Maybe your house simply works against you, not for you. You spend your time and energy accommodating the house. You walk extra steps every time you dress in the morning. You put up with a kitchen that barely functions. You tolerate a living room that never lets you relax and enjoy home life. What you need is a comfortable house.

House Comfortable is about how to make your home look, feel, and function flawlessly and conveniently. A well-designed home accomplishes a number of wide-ranging goals. It provides a safe haven from

Welcome to House Comfortable

1

the world, active space for family and solo activities, a work site for home offices, and a welcoming environment for entertaining.

When a home meets all these demands, it provides a successful background for living. Expect alterations in lifestyle such as marriage, a newly single status, new family members, or an empty nest to influence what will work for you and your house. *House Comfortable* anticipates tomorrow's lifestyle changes, but as lifestyles change over the course of the life cycle, one thing remains changeless: a need for comfort and a personal style that expresses the renewing spirit of home.

House Comfortable considers how the factors of aging and the potential for short- or long-term disability affect choices. Part of what has influenced *House Comfortable* is the coming of age of universal design, which takes into consideration differences in ability and bodily dimensions. Overall house, office, and public space design is conceived so that everyone has access. Appliances and furnishings are developed so that anyone, regardless of ability, can use them successfully. Universal design accommodates the needs of the young and old, the healthy and physically challenged. Why not consider all the potential needs for comfort and flexibility for everyone?

Within these pages lies comprehensive information and insights that will enhance your understanding of design—building or remodeling—and decoration. You will discover what is comfortable and how to furnish your home successfully. You will be equipped to analyze precisely what it is about your home that is uncomfortable. Then you will be able to correct the problems and achieve the results you want—your very own comfortable house. No matter what type of house you own or how it is decorated—plain or fancy, economically or extravagantly—it will look and feel completely right and natural.

The *House Comfortable* concept is a science and an art. What are the measurements, materials, and styles of comfortable living? What is the best couch for a couch potato? What kind of seating arrangements make conversation flow? How can a quieter, more peaceful kitchen be created? Are all the new features in high technology appliances worth the additional money? Making choices about furnishings, room arrangements, and even remodeling will be an easier process.

Knowing exactly the dimensions, features, and benefits you need *before* you enter a showroom or order from a catalog saves time, money, and energy. *House Comfortable* helps you to become your own expert on what is comfortable for you and then shows you how to find it. Certainly, purchasing the right furnishings and fixtures calls for lots of information and decision making. *House Comfortable* will help you hone your shopping skills.

House Comfortable means stress-free living. Tough work schedules and active lifestyles cry out for a house planning and design that makes living easier. Think of your house as a stress-free zone, clear of physical and emotional stressors, but dense with the restoring pleasures of home. All in all, such a house must be well conceived and executed, a task that requires self-knowledge, awareness of future needs, and information.

Often, homes just happen through hodgepodge furniture buying or happenstance changes, with no real planning at all. Home should be designed as a low-stress atmosphere that offers more than food, water, and shelter. Creature comforts such as big easy chairs promote a healthy, happy body, and psychological comforts like art or big-screen televisions address personal needs. An easy style appeals to all the senses and holds its value and beauty.

Comfort also plays a key role in health. The body demands physical and psychological comfort during work, play, or rest. At home, at the office, or in the car, our body reminds us in not-too-subtle ways that it must have a sympathetic environment.

Comfort issues in the workplace are addressed by federal legislation and insurance companies looking to cut costs of back strain and injury caused by a poorly designed environment. If you work on a PC, you have noticed that chair height, desk height, and position of the body affect overall health and performance. The study of *ergonomics* evaluates the way energy is expended and the overall effect it has on the body. How can employees expend the least amount of effort to accomplish their tasks and preserve their health and well-being? Companies study this question seriously.

How about applying some of this same thinking to the home? If you have to perform acrobatics to turn off the reading lamp or if you get a pain in the neck from watching TV in a spine-twisting position, then your body has already told you it's time to make some changes. If you have to leap over barricades of sofas and chairs to cross the room, heed your instincts and rearrange this mess. Perhaps one room blazes red hot in winter while another ices over. Your sense of temperature should give you a nudge. Fix the heating system, create comfort zones, and maybe rethink the kinds of materials used throughout the home.

A comfortable home recharges our physical and emotional batteries. The body demands restoration and relaxation. These processes are essential to repair muscles, take the burden off stressed joints, and give our little gray cells a chance to unwind. Eating, bathing, reading, watching television, knitting, all these are legitimately reconstructive activities that call for the sofas, chairs, and lamps that will provide *lasting comfort* to body and soul.

Many homeowners have come across the homes of their destiny. They report a feeling of encountering the ugliest house they have ever seen. *"It cried out to me for love"* is a common refrain. What they saw was potential, what they felt was their special ability to create beauty where there was precious little. They believed that the ugly house of reality could be—and would be—transformed into the house of their dreams.

Yet sometimes during this transformation process we become most concerned with formulas for figuring out if renovating our homes will pay off. If we remodel our kitchen and bath, will it be worth the expense down the road? So, with pencil and paper in hand, we estimate the costs, amortize them, figure them into the overall value of the house, and come up with a conclusion. Yes, we can increase our home's worth significantly, we reason. It is definitely worth the allocation of resources. But why not invest in every aspect of ourselves and not just our pocketbook?

It's difficult to determine the value of the more intangible aspects of home life. How will shaping our home into a paradise for our senses improve our lives? Sometimes we can only get a faint glimpse of the measure of happiness that an improvement might bring. Oftentimes, a change in the quality of life turns our lives around.

What is it about any room that makes us feel relaxed and cozy? If we know the answer to this question, we can successfully create an entire house that makes us feel good. We can also avoid the expensive mistakes of buying the wrong furniture or fabric or building cumbersome and inconvenient features into our kitchens, baths, bedrooms, and living rooms.

We will show you how to get great comfort into your home for a reasonable and affordable investment of time and energy. We will also show you how to make your house into a sanctuary and how to establish a true relationship between the house and its occupants. A home becomes comfortable only when it becomes our own unique world of happy memories and hopeful tomorrows. And, you know what? Comfort has never been more obtainable than right now.

The styles of comfort are two: country and contemporary eclectic. Style is not just determined by the way individual pieces are pulled together and placed in a room. Style is created through the subtle mixing of a variety of different design factors: color scheme, finishing materials, accessories, lighting, and the proportion and architecture of the rooms.

Country style and contemporary eclectic are the only approaches to interior decoration that look and feel inherently comfortable. Today, these two styles dominate the design world. Walk into just about any house in America and you will notice that the design concept is either country or contemporary. The furnishings of each meet the criteria of bodily comfort; that is, both styles encourage relaxation and express the unique personalities the inhabitants. Simplicity, ease, and a sense of free expression is the essence of comfortable style.

Country style is characterized by honest furnishings, natural materials, earth tone color schemes, plenty of texture, and everyday objects used as accessories. The design principle of country style means filling a room with lots of furniture, collected from various sources, upholstered in homespun florals, casual checks, and ginghams. Art depicts humble subjects or country scenes. There is an inventive use of available materials, an appreciation of things rustic, and a revival of the arcane. The look tends toward clutter and truly feels lived in. It is warm, welcoming, and natural.

What are the country styles? American, Swedish, English, and French and Italian Provincial are the most enduringly popular. The furniture designs of all these country style permutations are based on high styles that have been made less intimidating and more user-friendly. American country draws upon English and French styles. Swedish country is simplified French and Italian Provincial with liberal dollops of Swedish blue and yellow. French Provincial is a more rustic and heartier version of the all-too-refined Louis XV and XVI decorative arts. English country builds on French and Italian with lots of garden florals, more sensible construction, and a hundred-and-one portraits of dogs. Country style is unself-conscious and reveals its charm through an almost artless and never-ending accumulation of stuff.

Contemporary eclectic is the polar opposite of country style. It is

CHAPTER 1

The Comfortable Style

❧

Illustration opposite:
Country style

characterized by casual overstuffed furniture, few but important accessories, furniture only where you need it, and neutralized color schemes. Modular and sectional seating are good examples of this style's furniture mainstays. Contemporary eclectic emphasizes a casual take on modernist principles: *form follows function, less is more, the house is a machine for living.* Contemporary eclectic is self-conscious and tends toward lots of free space and clean lines. Every piece is placed just so. Lighting is used to emphasize points of interest. There may be lots of accessories or very few depending upon personal taste. Other influences may be present in the form of oriental rugs and so on. Technology and man-made materials are played up.

What Is Style?

Style expresses character and attitude. Some styles are intrinsically comfortable visually and physically, and others simply are not. Decorative styles have a distinctive design vocabulary that evokes a mood or feeling. When people feel a particular way, their behavior follows suit. For example, a formal dining room has upright chairs that encourage gracious manners; a den has upholstered couches for slouching.

Style is a matter of personality and intellectual interests. One particular style may better express *your* personality due to its perceived superiority of form or utility. Interiors *should* reflect personal style but at the same time they must be comfortable if they are to be functional. Individual style reflects your psyche. The focus today is on individuality versus conventionality.

Sometimes, a trendy look takes hold in our collective imagination. Fashion and decorating magazines devote pages and pages to it. Trends and fashions appreciate art for art's sake or, perhaps, trends for trends' sake, and they never take hold. Fashion is temporary, but style is enduring. Designers promote new ideas primarily to garner the attention of media. Trendy ideas are newsworthy, and that's what style editors at magazines and television shows are looking for. The look of the moment does what it is supposed to do: it appeals to the media and stimulates consumption. All designers in the decorative arts produce a few exam-

Illustration opposite:
Contemporary eclectic style

HOUSE
COMFORTABLE

ples of products that are *way out there*, thus forcing last season's fashions into extinction.

Not all fashion trends are without merit, however. Good fashions merge into the style of the period. Style, it is often said, transcends fashion. Don't decide on a particular style just because it is being done by someone, somewhere. Choose it because it is comfortable for you.

Generally, a style falls into the category of formal or informal. Formal and dressy styles place beauty, refinement, and aesthetics ahead of comfort. All the styles named after monarchs, for example, are formal. At-ease, dressed down, informal styles instead place comfort and function first and the look follows from there. If your stylistic preference is for more sophisticated and formalized decoration, it is possible to find furnishings that are designed for use and not just for looking pretty.

Period style is a definite trend in the character of architecture and decorative arts produced during a specific time in a specific place. Recognizable by the materials, forms, colors, and textures, each style was developed by social, economic, political, philosophical, scientific, and cultural influences. Keep in mind that the culture and technology that first produced your favorite style no longer exists. Don't let that fact keep you from buying it, but do buy period furniture that has been modified for today's bodies.

During their heyday, all period styles undergo an evolutionary development, reach a peak, and then fall into decline. A transition phase follows, and then a new style is born. Eventually, most period styles are rediscovered. Frequently, designers mine the past and reinvent a style by interpreting it for contemporary living.

A dialogue between intellect and emotion spurs evolutionary and revolutionary style development. Spiritual and material conditions such as new technology stimulate fresh creative directions. A new look is a reaction to the previous one: simple lines edge out complex curves, less casts out more, and so on. Take, for example, the designs of the Louis XV era, which were ornate and embellished with curvaceous motifs. The decorative philosophy of the subsequent Louis XVI period is based on clean lines and Greek and Roman aesthetic ideals. The two styles are opposites, but they followed each other back to back.

During the early twentieth century, all architecture and decorative art was based on predetermined style that merely imitated design ideas of the past. Style was reproduced without any originality, invention or understanding. The struggle to develop a modern idiom took hold during the period between the World Wars. Social mores broke down along with the rigidity of design. A willingness to cast aside all the old motifs and forms sent designers scrambling toward a more minimal design philosophy that favored utilitarianism and economy.

Comfort, perfect form, and minimal construction and materials were the criteria modernists employed when conceptualizing designs. They placed a great deal of emphasis on function and paid close attention to detail and proportion. Some designers hoped that these simplified furnishings would free the user's mind from all earthly thoughts so that he or she might focus on nobler things.

At "The Organic Design in Home Furnishings Exhibition" held at New York City's Museum of Modern Art in 1940, Charles Eames introduced his revolutionary furniture designs, which provided continuous support to the body (a first in furniture history!) while using a minimum of material. The Eames chair and other versions of it are now widely used in offices. You might say that more than fifty-five years later, comfort has come of age.

Although designers of modern houses and furniture thought a great deal about issues of comfort, their designs looked intellectual and cold. Too much abstraction fails to look comfortable and cozy. However, many of the innovations and variations of modernist designs can be used in relaxed and free-spirited contemporary eclectic homes.

If you plan to include furniture from historic styles and periods in your home, use country or provincial styles and not the strictly formal urban forms. Provincial versions of period styles fit nicely into today's relaxed rooms. How can you spot a provincial version of a formal style? The provincial or country interpretation of formal furniture will look more squat, robust, and chunky. The proportions will probably appear awkward even to an untrained eye. These more generously scaled pieces look friendly and are upholstered in dressed-down linens, cottons, or synthetics. Provincial French and Italian chairs and Scandinavian furniture based on French and Italian styles mix very easily with more contemporary sofas.

Fortunately, there are styles of furniture and decorative looks designed with solid comfort in mind. These include Arts and Crafts (and its offspring mission style), Biedermeir, contemporary, modern, American Colonial, and all the provincial and country styles of America and Europe.

A general style theme should prevail throughout the house. Using one style in one room and another in the next will look disjointed. Let your house, the region where you live, and your taste inform your choice of style. *House Comfortable* style is not a draw-within-the-lines approach to furnishing. It is a framework for the canvas of your home.

By selecting your color scheme, furniture styles, upholstery, accessories, materials, and finishes, you will produce the look you want. Elsie de Wolf, a breakthrough decorator of the twentieth century, updated her dark, Victorian-style New York apartment simply by painting wood furniture and wood trim white and taking all artwork off the walls and tossing out all the objets d'art and bric-a-brac. Presto! Without buying a stick of furniture or changing the wallpaper, she went from one style to another.

Getting the look you want starts with knowing what you like and who you are. Country types prefer Laura Ashley and Mario Buatta; contemporary eclectics like Calvin Klein. Tear out all the magazine pictures of rooms you like. Collect them in a folder. Take note of all the furnishings you love and what it is that attracts you to a particular room. Jot down a list of the architectural details (moldings, windows, fireplaces, and doors) you like. These notes, sketches, snapshots of your own house and rooms, and information about your floor plan should be kept together in a folder that you can take on shopping trips. You may want to share your notes with a decorator or designer who can help you come up with inventive solutions. Remember, the more you understand your personal sense of style, the better and more comfortable your home will be.

CHAPTER 2

The Color of Comfort

In a comfortable house, color plays a key role. Color expresses character. As we enter a home and move through its rooms, we should sense an overall, unifying color theme that establishes mood and tone. Rooms should flow naturally together to create a sense of wholeness. One room's colors should relate to the function of the room, as well as to the rest of the home. Any successful color scheme ultimately involves the entire house.

The *problem* of color selection is to develop a pleasing harmony that produces a desirable psychological and emotional reaction, yet at the same time suits the function of the room and relates well with the quality of the natural and artificial light. There are also a host of additional considerations to keep in mind when making your color selection: the size of the room and its proportions, the amount of uninterrupted space, the textures of its surfaces, the relation of colors to each other, and the dimensions of the furnishings.

A comfortable color scheme is based on neutrals and neutralized colors that look to nature as their source. Neutralized colors work with a wide assortment of other colors, from subdued to bright. Successful color strategies create an easygoing atmosphere, no matter how formal or informal the room's character. Neutrals go from day to night, season to season, year to year. Neutrals always look good and function well.

The neutrals are easy-to-live-with colors. They calm rather than excite, ease tensions rather than build them. Color schemes drawn from a palette of neutrals create a perfect backdrop for living. From a decorative standpoint, neutrals and neutralized colors look polished and put-together while expressing a relaxed intimacy and warmth. The truest neutrals like gray, from slate to smoke, look a bit more formal, while neutralized and subdued browns, beiges, and tans are more easygoing.

Selecting your neutral scheme depends upon the character you want your room to convey. Character, which describes the mood, tone, and feeling of a color, relates an overall aesthetic and psychological statement that can usually be described as refreshing, posh, country, woodsy, natural, cheerful, sober, feminine, or masculine.

A phrase that won't come up is "drop-dead glamour"—the look of the '70s and '80s. This is a relentless, tiring, and alienating style that screams conspicuous consumption. If glamour and drama is what you want, it can be achieved in the newest neutrals that are livable, vital, and—dare we say?—tasteful.

Our response to color is partly instinctual and natural and partly learned and cultural. Color has innate meaning and creates a strong natural response from within us. City living pays no heed to day or night, to the passage of seasons, yet city dwellers continue to respond to the natural world. Preferences for colors change with age, education, and socioeconomic status, but it seems the older, wealthier, and more experienced someone is, the more likely that person is to choose neutralized colors that calm and soothe. Toddlers love purple and glitter, for example, while their more sophisticated grade school siblings with allowance money prefer red and blue.

The neutral color planning of a comfortable house starts with an observation of nature and its use of color. Nature has its own way of organizing colors. In general, the ground is dark (green, brown), the sky lighter (ranging gray to blue), and the area surrounding the horizon line is of medium value and low intensity.

There are ways of thinking about natural color relationships and how we relate to them. The four seasons symbolically represent periods of activity and inactivity, beginnings and endings. Winter is a time for stillness. Its landscape is a study in shades of grays, from blue gray (cool) to brown gray (warm). The landscape of spring is pale, clear, and warmed by yellows, tender greens, and softened earth tones. It is a time for beginnings.

Summer's sky is markedly blue violet, the green is strong and deeper in value, and the contrast between sky and ground is firm. It is a time for growth. Autumn is a study in complement and contrast, and its distinctive palette ranges from bright reds to deep shades of russet, wine, and brown. It is a time for endings and beginnings: the Jewish New Year begins in fall, as does the new school year and many new marriages (October is the second favorite month for weddings next to June).

Color exerts a physiological and psychological force. Psychologists who study color explain that reactions to color are universal. For example, the dark blue environment of night depresses the nervous system and cues the body for sleep. Dark blue also represents depth of feeling and engenders tranquillity, contentment, tenderness, love, and affection.

Navy blue is the color of choice for major blue-chip companies. Day, with its yellow rays of sunshine, excites the nervous system and preps the body for action. Yellow represents spontaneity and is expansive and inspiring. It elicits emotions that are variable and expectant and increases originality and feelings of exhilaration.

Some colors produce feelings related to the flight or fight states. Red, the color of blood, is stimulating and suggests an attack. It is known to increase circulation and heartbeat and is used in dining rooms and exercise rooms. Some consider it a sexy color. Green, on the other hand, slows down heart rate and is associated with healing. Muted shades of green are widely used in hospitals and dispensaries. During the 1950s, many designers hyped its balanced character.

Green also connotes willfulness. Its effect is to increase persistence, self-assertion, obstinacy, and it reinforces self-esteem. Hunter green is a traditional color of the decor of men's clubs.

Colors also have traditional symbolic meanings. White suggests peace, purity, faith, joy, and cleanliness. Red symbolizes passion, anger, warmth, gaiety, martyrdom, and revolution. Blue evokes restfulness, coolness, constancy, truth, and reliability. The American flag is red, white, and blue. Deep blue is the Virgin Mary's color. Black is the polar opposite of white and represents darkness, despair, sorrow, and mourning. Green traditionally recalls spring, hope, restfulness, and coolness. Yellow conjures up warmth, cheerfulness, and fruitfulness.

Somber gray symbolizes humility and penance and has been favored by such diverse groups as Puritans and Maoist Chinese. Purple, an expensive color to produce in ancient times, has come to mean justice or royalty, as well as depression and suffering. It is also a liturgical color in Christian churches. Gold stands for royalty, luxury, and power, and it frequently shows up in bathrooms as a strong accent color.

Trends in colors and color schemes generally experience an overhaul every three years. Over the course of a decade, that means three dominant color trends will be seen, and perhaps one particular color will come to typify the age. That is not such a bad thing if the color scheme is relaxing and beautiful, but because color calls for an investment of precious resources, it's best to learn which color schemes work best for you. Corporations pick their schemes carefully.

Color is logical. A good color sense is not a matter of instinct, but it can be developed. You need not be born under a special star to have a good sense of color, nor do you have to be especially aesthetically inclined. All humans have a built-in color sense that needs only to be brought forth through experience and education.

A discussion of the practical use of color begins with an examination of the theory of color. Color has five characteristics: hue, value, intensity, temperature, and finish. Hue is the attribute by which we recognize and describe a color, the color name. Blue is blue, whether it is sky blue or midnight blue; the difference is the value. Value is the degree of lightness or darkness. Intensity, or chroma, refers to the relative purity or saturation of the hue. A high intensity is a pure or almost pure shade. A low intensity is a neutralized shade. Temperature refers to the way in which colors either advance (warm) or recede (cool). All colors have a surface or finish, from shiny to matte, that interacts with light and thus alters our perception of it.

Natural color relationships are most easily described in terms of the color wheel. A color wheel is essentially refracted light (like the rainbow) bent into a circle. The order of color runs from the longer wavelengths of red, orange, and yellow (the warm colors) to the shorter wavelengths of green, blue, and violet (the cool colors). Although you can perceive hundreds of thousands of colors, every color is simply a blend of the three primaries (red, blue, and yellow) with white or black added in.

If you were to examine a color wheel, you will notice that colors have relationships to one another. Colors found next to each other are analogous. Colors placed opposite each other are complementary. Mixing two complementary colors produces a neutral. The wheel is also halved down the middle: on the right side are the warm colors, on the left are the cool colors. Working with the wheel can be helpful, and most color schemes make use of a color wheel relationship. Oftentimes, you can find a workable color wheel in the consumer literature supplied by paint companies at your local paint store, or you can purchase one in any art supply store.

Analyzing interiors you love in terms of the designated color scheme will increase your understanding of why some color combinations have a particular impact and why some other interiors fail to have the desired effect. The eight basic color stories are:

1. *Monotone neutral color scheme:* One single low chroma in one value or in a limited range of values is used on floor, walls, ceiling, and everything else. Think whites, grays, beiges, taupes. A good example is the all-white room. Once a startling statement maker, the all-white room is a standard, especially in contemporary homes.

2. *Monochromatic color scheme:* Select one color and work with different values and chroma. Camel to brown (all variations on orange) is one such story. Softened rose tones and tints are very feminine. Three or four values of gray also look smart. Work with paints on a single color strip and pick a subdued color for best results.

3. *Analogous color scheme:* Select three colors that lie next to each other on the wheel. Then, span only one-quarter of the color wheel and select subdued shades or subtle tints of your chosen colors. A grey blue plus neutralized blue violet and blue green is an example. Yellow, green, and blue is another plan. The yellows in wood teamed with pale, atmospheric blue gray fieldstone flooring with celadon accents is relaxing. Remember, tints and shades expand the analogous color scheme.

4. *Complementary color scheme:* Choose two colors opposite one another on the color wheel. One will be warm, the other cool, and one should dominate the other. Stick to subdued values of color. This combination inherently builds tension. Typical pairs include red and green in the form of burgundy and hunter green, rosy pink and teal, orange and blue in their neutral forms of tan and slate, and yellow and violet dressed as gold and plum.

5. *Split-complement color scheme:* Select one main color and two almost-but-not-quite complementary colors to accompany it. The classic example is red teamed with yellow green and blue green, the two complements that lie beside green. The largest area should be a low-intensity color. The two split complements

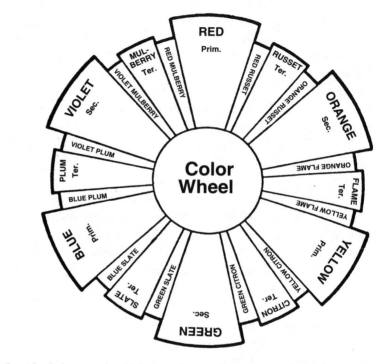

Color wheel showing the 24 basic colors in their proper relationship. Colors that are complementary are opposite each other. Analagous colors are placed next to each other. Warm colors are found on the right side of the wheel; cool colors are found on the left side of the wheel.

can be more intense in saturation and should be used in smaller areas and as accents. Effective split-complementary color stories can be more subtle and cheerful than a simple complementary one.

6. *Alternate complement color scheme:* Pick a color. Find its complement, then select a color two paces to the left and another one two paces to the right. Let us say flame, a yellow orange yellow, is the main color. Team it with its complement, plum, and its cousins, violet and blue. How would that work in real life? A palest tint of flame (an apricot-tinged white) for walls, a grayed blue carpet, patterned upholstery and drapes, with accents of violet or lavender. Remember, use subdued tints or shades, not the high-density true colors.

7. *Triad color scheme:* Opt for three colors equidistant on the wheel. A major triad is red, yellow, and blue (the Brillo box is an example). A minor triad is orange, green, and violet. Triads are frequently executed in saturated colors for fun, vivid looks. Often, a neutral, such as the floor, acts as a background for the triad. Even low-chroma variations look lively and are good for children's rooms.

8. *Tetrad color scheme:* Tetrad is composed of four equally spaced hues picked from around the wheel. Red, yellow, green, and blue in very subdued shades can generate a familiar and traditional feel. Tetrads are trickier to handle than most schemes.

Color is never seen by itself. It is always perceived in relation to something else and in the context of light and shadow. Complementary colors placed next to each other create tension. Colors placed in relation to black or white change, becoming more or less intense. Placing a hue in black surroundings makes it appear more saturated; white surroundings have the opposite effect. Small areas of color placed side by side create the illusion of many more colors than are actually present. The farther away a color is, the lighter the value appears to be.

The effect of color on form and space can be exploited to make an interior seem like more or less than it is. Warm hues and high-intensity colors are visually active and stimulating. Cool hues and low-intensity colors are subdued and relaxing. Light values are cheerful, middle values undemanding, dark values somber. Deep, cool colors contract: an object looks smaller. Light, warm colors expand: an object looks bigger. Understanding the impact of color and obeying these natural, immutable rules insures success and prevents costly mistakes. When something does go wrong with our color schemes, we can refer to the rules to discover which ones we've broken and alter our scheme accordingly.

What's Your Color Strategy?

House Comfortable uses a practical approach to color story development. The steps are methodical and logical. Doing your homework before making major color decisions will save you disappointment and frustration. It will also go a long way toward creating a successful interior design.

There are almost always some limitations imposed upon the design of a room: certain pieces of furniture must be used, the flooring won't be changed, the lighting can't be changed. Instead of seeing a forced situation as a prison (the hateful russet leather furniture is staying!), see it as an opportunity. Get out your color wheel and play with the eight types of color schemes. Try out the configurations. Will using low chromas and deeper values make the russet blend into the room's overall decor? Will adding complements or analogous hues distract from the overly aggressive orange red? You have nothing to lose by experimenting with a set of color chips or samples.

If you are not happy with your own efforts, or if you want to take a shortcut, go to your favorite fabric shop. Look for suitable fabrics that feature as a dominant color the dreaded russet that you are trying to conquer. We guarantee that you will come away with several good choices. Study the color combinations that the textile artists have devised. You will probably be amazed and delighted with the variety and inspired by the possibilities that are yours to borrow. These experts work with color—they are our best teachers when it comes to identifying soul-satisfying color relationships.

The character of your rooms should guide you as you select your color story. More subdued rooms will probably be best in simpler color schemes, and playful rooms will call for more active application of colors. Keep your color story relatively limited: one, two, or three colors is all you need. With variations in tints and shades, it is conceivable that one color story could thread its way through your entire home.

Don't be afraid of color, just be sure to carefully visualize the effect, get feedback from family members, and ultimately rely on both your knowledge and your instincts. Retailers usually offer large-sized samples of upholstery, wallpaper, and carpeting to take home. It is important to see how the color will look in a particular room in your house.

When considering wallpaper, order a large-sized, two-foot-square sample. The charge for the sample is minimal (about $5 or so), and usually it can be applied toward your purchase. Wallpaper stores recommend that the piece be taped to the wall and lived with for twenty-four hours to see how it looks under different lights. The larger size will let you see the effect of any stripes and patterns. Often just looking at the page in a book will not give you enough information to make a decision. You need to take the extra time and steps, given the cost of paper and installation.

If worst comes to worst, you can purchase a small container of puce or pimpernel or whatever daring color you're considering. Paint a small section of a wall to see how it offsets the basic neutrals in the rooms. Paint, even wild colors, can be painted over if need be, and most paints are not generally too expensive, particularly if you are doing it yourself. There are many books on how to paint utilizing various techniques like faux finishes, striae, combing, and sponging. These techniques can add interest and keep the color subdued. An experienced paint pro, if you will be hiring one to do the final job, can also recommend colors, finishes, and special effects.

The general rule of thumb for any color story is the *law of chromatic distribution*: larger areas should be covered in the most neutralized colors of the scheme; as areas reduce in size, the chromatic intensity may be proportionately increased.

Start by picking a neutralized chroma for the floor. Floors may be a lighter or darker value than the walls and ceiling. The traditional scheme, derived from nature, is to designate the floor as a relatively deeper value than medium-value walls and light-value ceiling. In most cases in the home, you will want to avoid overly contrasting values, which will make the space choppy and ugly. Think in terms of relating the floor's value to the walls. The floor should be somewhat deeper in value than the walls, and deeper still compared to the ceiling. This holds true even if you are using light values of camel or beige.

There are times you may want to keep the values of floor, wall, and ceiling close. An all-white (or off-white) scheme, for example, makes an expansive and cooling backdrop for other neutrals to come into play. Many contemporary homes in sunny climes feature ceramic tiles in solid white or with a subtle veining of color with soaring white cathedral ceilings. All light values make the most of volume and look contemporary.

In general, tonal variation is pleasing. Secondary elements, like furniture and area rugs, can take more chromatic intensity. Small-scale pieces command more attention when they are dressed in a stronger chroma. Offset large areas of light value with smaller areas of medium and dark.

Keep in mind that as colors are introduced into the scheme, sufficient repetition of the color is necessary. Just one splash of color may say very little; repeating it throughout a room is much more effective. Repetition of color creates a motif and establishes a logic. If the accent color is an acid green throw pillow, for example, you may want to use three or more on the sofa and pick up the color again in the artwork or some other accessory. Something to avoid, on the other hand, is the equal distribution of color—one-half the room is red, the other green—as it tends to create too much tension. Use the law of chromatic distribution. It works.

The current trends in design favor a warm color palette that features yellow, warm greens, browns, and reds inspired by nature. Cool blues and grays provide balance. Metals and minerals are emerging in paints, finishes, and fabrics. Copper, granite, jade, and amethyst are favorites for countertops. Texture is also important; it creates depth, warmth, and coziness. In wall paint, sheer color-over-color glazes can be used on walls to give more dimension. Any combination of colors can be used for a desired effect.

Color can be used to emphasize or de-emphasize a room's basic features. The basic rules of color theory can be applied to maximize a room's potential or correct a room's flaws. To alter a room's apparent dimensions, use the basic science of advancing and receding colors. The following tips will help you modify apparent size, shape, scale, and distance:

- To increase apparent space, use monochromatic, light, cool color schemes to create a receding atmosphere. Paint all surfaces the same color and match the upholstery to the floor.
- To make a ceiling look higher, use white or the same color as the walls, and keep floors relatively light.
- To reduce the apparent space, use darker, warmer, low-chroma shades. Employ a dado (a decorative element that creates a division between upper and lower walls), wainscoting, or molding to create panels in a contrasting paint. Light, middle, or deep values may be used for the walls. Molding may match or contrast.
- To square off a long room, use a cool tint on the long, narrow wall and a dark, warm color on the short end.
- To narrow a wide room, use a deeper, low-chroma value on long walls and lighter-value, cool tints on the shorter walls.
- Black out an ugly ceiling with black, dark gray, or midnight blue.

Hints for a Successful Color Story

1. Neutral color schemes are the most comfortable.
2. The largest areas (walls, floors, and ceilings) should be a livable neutral color.
3. The second largest area (furniture, other finishes) should be a neutral (the same color or a different value light or dark) or neutralized color.
4. Spice up the smallest areas with bright accent colors.
5. Limit your color scheme to a maximum of three colors.
6. Carry your color scheme throughout the house.
7. To easily harmonize any color scheme, choose colors that approach each other on the color wheel.
8. Use enough contrast in color and value to create interest.
9. If using a monotone neutral, add interest with texture, pattern, and important accessories.

THE
COLOR OF
COMFORT

Three Steps for Creating Your Color Scheme

To find the best colors and textures for a particular room in your home, use this guide to help you gather information. This data can be recorded as part of the process of creating a floor plan, which we will discuss further in chapter seven.

Step one: Answer these basic questions:

- What geographic region do you live in?
- Is the style of your home contemporary or country?
- What is the orientation of the room's windows?
- How much daylight is allowed into the room?
- Does the room receive morning or afternoon sun or both?
- Where is the artificial lighting located in the room?
- What are the main functions of the room?
- During what hours will the space will be used?
- Who will be using the room? What colors do they like?
- How would you describe the atmosphere you are trying to create?
- What are the general proportions of the room?
- Does the room seem to need visual correction?
- What are the features of the room that can't be changed (furniture, floor, etc.)?

Step two: Set the tone. Find the best neutrals and the neutralized colors for your room based on the facts you gathered in step one.

- Which dominant colors in the room can't be changed?
- Does the room need warm neutrals?

- Does the room need cool neutrals?
- Taking into account the purpose of the room and the times of the day it is used, are lighter, middle, or darker values the best choices?
- Which features of the room should be emphasized?
- Which features should be de-emphasized?

Step three: Collect a variety of flooring and wall covering samples, paint chips, upholstery, and window treatment fabrics from within your color scheme. Make selections of color for the major large areas:

- Floor
- Walls
- Ceiling

Then, add colors for secondary areas:

- Upholstery
- Window treatments
- Area rugs

Add accent colors:

- Art and art objects
- Accessories (pillows, throws, etc.)

Decorating is a process that involves gathering information, making decisions, and then orchestrating everything that needs to be done—all within a reasonable framework of time. To make the process go smoothly, *House Comfortable* lays out the tasks in broad steps, first addressing what needs to be done before the decorating and furnishing steps are undertaken.

Comfortable Design

Design is the product of individual expression. Your home ought to be decorated with what you love, tempered by regard for the natural rules of color, texture, and relationship between objects. Making your house comfortable calls for decorating with common sense. There is an enormous array of products in the marketplace. Don't run out and buy the first thing you see just to get the job done. Be patient. Be willing to explore. Do not try to plan to the very last detail. Leave plenty of sketchy areas to be filled in as you go.

Decorating is vision that starts off fuzzy and imprecise. It is like looking at a scene from a long distance. The closer you get, the more you see. You could not have envisioned or imagined all the details. You could not have known they even existed. Trying to anticipate every little detail is stressful. By predetermining every last detail, you end up eliminating serendipity and surprise. Decorating is a spiritual as well as a practical task that is rewarding and fun. Looking along the way for the unimagined and unanticipated is part of the excitement and enjoyment. Finding things along the way is interesting. The shopping process should be fun.

This is general advice. Now let's be specific. Say, for example, you know you like a rustic style and muted colors. You envision a setting. You select blue gray barn board as a wall covering. Decide what types of sofas and chairs you'll need for the room and where they will be placed for comfort and convenience. At this point, don't try to decide which chairs will be checked, striped, plain, or plaid. Most rooms have only one optimal layout. The size and shape of the room will also dictate the scale of furnishings. The architecture has a character and there are only a few stylistic approaches that will seem appropriate.

CHAPTER 3

Creating Comfortable Backgrounds

Once you've determined the placement of furniture, you may go to the next step, shopping for fabric samples. Gather up a variety of fabric swatches in all the patterns and colors that interest you and seem to work together. Bring back all the suitable samples, along with a sample of the barn board, and lay it all out in the room.

How do the fabrics look with the barn board in this room? Which look good together? Make decisions by a process of elimination. Let's say you brought back seven fabrics from the stores you have visited. You will need three to four. You will see, by placing the samples together in various combinations, which ones work and which ones do not.

Designers use this same process. It's called *the vague vision method*. They gather up the possibilities, then make comparisons. They shuffle and eliminate until they find the very best choices. The vague vision approach starts with a big picture, leaves lots of room for discovery, and lets you have fun playing the field.

Another approach to successful decorating is *the jigsaw puzzle method*. Begin with the one thing you love—a favorite sofa or a rug—and then add other elements until all the pieces of the puzzle are in place.

Let us imagine that you have a glorious rug. The pattern, color, mood, and overall design has a message. Sort through all your fabric choices to find upholstery for your sofa and chairs that suits the mood of your rug. The other elements will then fall into place. Wall coverings, window treatments, and accessories should relate logically to the rug. All you have to do is judge how well things fit together. When elements are compatible, they enhance each other. If the other elements become more important than the primary element (the thing you love, whatever it may be), confusion will result. If the various decorative components of your room compete, you have made a mistake. Keep the design focus on the thing you love, the jigsaw piece that is at the center of your design puzzle. Everything else is subordinate.

The better-safe-than-sorry method is another approach to decorating. Pick conservative neutrals and traditional patterns as backgrounds, and stick with traditional furniture styles. Play it safe with the major elements. Take risks by buying splashy accessories that can be changed seasonally or simply discarded. Safe choices are not necessarily boring. They are comfortable and livable. Beiges, tans, white, white/black, and gray are reliable choices. Pay special attention to quality and durability. The better the materials, the better the results. If you relocate frequently or plan a drastic move in the future, the better-safe-than-sorry approach is the way to go.

Decorating for comfort is a rational process. It is a little like knowing you need to buy an evening dress for an event. You know the basic requirements: long, dressy, formal in feeling, and costing no more than your budget allows. The field is narrowed to eliminate items that do not meet your criteria, but it remains open enough to consider a host of styles. The dress—or the decor—you ultimately select should be a reflection of your taste.

Taste

"Taste," said the late design educator Sherrill Whiton, "is not necessarily a product of gentility of birth, intellect, or opulence; but it usually grows on the top branches of the trees of culture and refinement, and it is part of an instinct that is reflected in the words, actions, and creative efforts of an individual."

Taste is an ability to discern good, better, and best. Taste is learned and comes about through education, experience, and understanding of aesthetics. It includes a sensitivity that enables one to tell the true from the false.

Taste, rather than being flat and studied, is imbued with personality and expression. It is evidenced in the grouping, proportion, and composition of a design. It is not necessarily the by-product of a big budget. Interiors, like Hollywood movies, tend to benefit from being limited to a budget. Taste and beauty are often found in simple and inexpensive settings where there is an orderly arrangement of details that suits the function and design of the room.

The ideal of taste is to make every room look natural and as though it is used by someone who enjoys it. All human beings differ, and our interiors should reflect these differences. There should be an absence of self-consciousness and too much correctness, an avoidance of the preconceived and packaged. Every object should have a reason for being.

Taste and individuality are the intangible essentials that distinguish the extraordinary from the ordinary. While all rooms should focus on the functional and the practical, the expression of the personality of the inhabitants must never be lost. Discard the notion that taste means boring and static and snooty. Taste is for you and me and everyone.

Design

There are also three design notions prevalent today that, if adhered to, are guaranteed to have unpleasant effects. Many of these ideas are expressed in decorating and women's magazines:

• Have It Your Way

This concept is great for burgers, but not for interiors. Behind the notion of *have it your way* is the idea that whatever you see and like is automatically right and that everything you like works together perfectly. Wrong! By experience, you already know this is a surefire way to produce a lousy wardrobe. Ditto for the home. Colors and patterns that depart from your scheme only serve to create confusion and disharmony. Piling on more and more extraneous colors and elements fails to make a design statement. The *have it your way* approach to spontaneous decorating may help someone reach a sales quota for the day, but it will not help you comfortably furnish your home.

• Anything Goes

If you believe that anything goes, you think you do not need to know about periods and styles; everything goes together in the so-called eclectic decor. Go right ahead, buy a Stickley chair to go with a faux Queen Anne and contemporary Italian, the theory goes, and it will all look wonderful. After all, the decor is eclectic, isn't it?

Eclectic decor, far from being a free-for-all approach, must display a strong, unifying design principle. Typically, to be successfully eclectic, the room's decor must predominantly be one period style with only one piece of furniture from a contrasting style. There must be a design relationship between the two styles. If not, the result is unsatisfyingly junky. Mixed periods and styles—the anything goes look—is seldom wonderful.

• Design Anarchy

Design anarchy says you should actively break all of the tried-but-true design rules and challenge authority like a rebellious teenager. This notion involves thinking that you never need to consult a professional before making a decision, nor do you ever need to take any advice. You should question authority, it says, and flaunt your ignorance while flouting all the rules. In result, your rooms will look identical to your teenager's and probably end up reflecting all the shopworn conventions you were so desperately trying to avoid.

Adhering to these notions means believing you have nothing to learn and you need learn nothing to decorate successfully. There is always *something* to learn about yourself and your tastes, and a decorator or designer can offer a great deal of insight and guidance. Do not be shy about consulting a qualified specialist who will work with you and even tell you when you are wrong.

Design Principles

Before turning to the chapters on specifics, let's get an overview of *good* design principles. The following are some very basic design concepts or rules.

• Composition

All design needs contrast and variety. A *design* is an orderly arrangement of lines, forms, masses, colors, or textures, forming a unified composition. Design, to be successful, must command interest primarily through the introduction of contrast and movement. Any design without contrast is flat and static. An excess of contrast or movement lacks unity, grows confusing, and tires the observer.

• Line

Straight lines come in three varieties: vertical, horizontal, and diagonal. Straight lines are static; curved lines create movement. Vertical lines force the eye to move from top to bottom, producing an attention attitude. Horizontal lines draw the eye side to side and instill a restful response. Diagonal lines suggest active movement forward.

Much of our perception of what a line means comes from our own physical experience. Lying down, we are in a horizontal pose and at rest. Standing up, we are awake and alert. When we are running, we are propelling our bodies through space on a diagonal.

• Mass

The mass of furniture must relate successfully to the space it occupies and to each other piece in the group. Small, spindly pieces of furniture will look inadequate and silly in a huge room. Overly large pieces crammed into a tiny apartment will look a little ungainly.

• Judgment

You must make informed judgments about introducing the proper amount of contrast and movement into a room to avoid the extremes of dullness and confusion. *Texture*, *color*, and patterns must be creatively and adroitly used. Too much texture, color, and pattern can look confused and confusing. Too little, on the other hand, is unsatisfyingly boring.

• Proportion

Proportion addresses the relationship of the parts of the design to the whole. It is not hard to tell bad proportions from good. Bad proportions simply look wrong and unsettling. Good proportions look satisfying. It's easier to recognize good proportions than to achieve them.

• Balance

Balanced design looks comfortable and may be achieved either through striving for *symmetry* or *asymmetry*. Our eyes are most accustomed to bilateral symmetry, in which the right side looks just like the left. Historic buildings are usually based on this principle. Asymmetrical balance establishes equilibrium between two unequal elements. Different elements of different weights can balance each other through placement or variation in shape, color, and size.

• Rhythm

Rhythm relates visual elements in a regular pattern. Architectural features such as windows or columns create rhythmic systems. Furnishings and finishes that repeat a pattern or motif establish rhythm in an interior.

• **The Key Element**

Emphasis of a key design element is essential. Every room must have a main focus. Everything else is subordinate to that main element. If every feature in a room is of equal importance, then nothing is important.

• **Pattern and Ornamentation**

To enliven a surface and establish mood, introduce pattern and ornamentation. Not all rooms need embellishment. Some rooms are based on a spare aesthetic. Modern and contemporary styles generally use ornamentation with restraint. Care must be taken to avoid excess ornamentation and pattern. Other styles, such as Victorian and country, need some tasteful clutter.

The Final Touch

No one is perfect. Neither is any interior. Any room and, for that matter, any house, is a product of your imagination. There is a living and dynamic quality to a comfortable room that allows for minor (or even major) changes, revisions, additions, and perhaps an occasional deletion of a detail. As your life grows, so does your home.

Leave a little room for growing space. You don't have to set about totally finishing a room, filling all wall space, using every inch of display space. Think instead of filling in the major brush strokes first, adding details when you can. Every room needs breathing space.

Not every single thing in a room has to match. A room can harmoniously accommodate some dissonance if attention is paid to the overall principles of design. Sister Parish, a great decorator, would paint mismatched styles of dark wood furniture a sparkling white, bringing them into harmony. Another decorating magazine stylist consciously included in her room settings a single item that was a mistake in order to create a feeling of real life. Although we aim for unity in a comfortable interior, one or two serendipitous elements add a welcome relief and a human quality that everyone can appreciate. And, while we aim for some degree of perfection, we want to avoid artificiality. It's unreal and uncomfortable.

CHAPTER 4

Quiet!

No wonder the National Bureau of Standards says American homes are too noisy. Acoustics experts note that the comfort level of human hearing is at about forty to fifty decibels, but the typical home has an ambient sound level of fifty decibels or more. Yikes! High levels of sound create confusion, stress, illness, and, according to a recent medical finding, premature babies. Noise, which is unwanted sound, creates physical and psychological irritation. While we can tune out or ignore loud noise, there is little we can do to stop the stress it produces. Noises louder than eighty-five decibels (from, for example, poorly installed, low-grade dishwashers) cause headaches, hearing loss, and stress-related illness.

Hushing the rattle and hum of your home and office increases well-being, improves communication, and enhances listening pleasure. As we grow older, our hearing diminishes: higher pitched sounds can't be heard, and sounds are harder to distinguish. Conversation, even if it is loud, can be hard to hear above the din of ambient sound. Reducing noise by five to ten decibels inside the home can make a positive difference. To control noise, loud rooms must be separated from quiet ones. You can control the way sound travels in your house through choosing materials and finishes that absorb sound.

About Sound

Lots of data comes to us through hearing. What we hear is an important part of our waking experience and even appears to us in dreams as aural symbols. Notice the number of descriptive words for sounds produced by nature (thunder, roar, whistle, patter, rippling) and the animal kingdom (bark, meow, snarl, growl, chirp). Humans, not content with the limitless reverberations of the natural world, have invented yet more sounds, from the rattle of machinery to the booming bass of music.

In its pure scientific form, the study of sound is a branch of physics and is therefore subject to mathematical analysis. Sound in a laboratory is one thing, but it is completely another thing in the real world. We can not stop cars from zooming through our neighborhoods. There is not much that can be done to stop air traffic overhead. However, we can dampen down irritating sounds to tolerable levels.

The Science of Sound

For how to live with sound, we turn to acoustics, the science that studies how sound acts in real life and in real places. All the scientific data collected through the study of acoustics helps engineers, architects, and designers control sound. Without consideration given to noise reduction in the initial stages of design, life at home and at the office would be intolerable. Basic understanding of sound makes planning a home easier. Layout, fabrics, finishing materials, and other equipment also can influence sound transmission.

Sound bends around corners (this is called diffraction), travels through any material, and moves fastest through liquids and solids and slowest through air. It grows louder in a closed room (a product of reverberation, reflection, and resonance), changes its pitch if the sound wave is traveling toward you or away from you (the Doppler effect), or is silenced though the phenomenon of interference.

Sound is a compression wave. We hear frequency as pitch. Magnitude refers to loudness or softness. When two or more notes are blended together, they reinforce each other at some points and cancel each other out at others, resulting in a third unique sound. All these factors combined with real-world factors such as temperature and materials provide quite a bit to anticipate during the designing and decorating process.

Some reverberation of sound is ideal. A reverberation period of one second, according to scientist Isaac Asimov, is the aim of most acoustic design. Without it, sound has a flat, dead quality. Some spaces of the home, like the home theater room, will need careful acoustic design. Others may need special sound dampening materials and construction techniques.

The most striking characteristic of sound is how it bends around objects and continues to travel until it is slowed by friction. Sound waves diffract much more than light. Only a fraction of a light wave can peek around a corner, but most of a sound wave will travel uninterrupted. Since sound travels in compression waves, it acts upon air somewhat like ripples in water. When sound waves smack into a surface, the waves try to set the object in motion. When they succeed, sound travels on— through floors, walls, and ceilings. If the wave is bigger than the obstacle it encounters, it slips right around the barrier undeterred. When it fails to pass around or set the object vibrating, the wave energy is transformed to a minuscule amount of heat. The result is silence.

Designs to Block Sound

What makes a house so noisy? Unwanted sounds from exterior and interior sources bend around and bounce off objects. Outside, car, air, and train traffic and noisy power tools are to blame. Inside, *airborne noise* and *impact noise* create racket. Appliances, especially several operating at the same time (running water, TV, and the dishwasher to name a few), and conversation are typical sources of airborne noise. Footfalls from people and pets are responsible for impact noise.

Controlling noise is well worth the effort. In cases where noise can be reduced but not eliminated, try introducing what is called acoustic perfume. Consider masking the offensive noise with a pleasant sound. A water fountain situated in an outdoor garden masks traffic noise. But in most households, noise reduction is the goal.

The higher the pitch of a sound, the shorter its wave and the more easily deflected it is by building materials. Low pitched sounds are low frequency and slip around barriers and travel through material. That is why the thudding bass booms of a passing car with a souped-up stereo system are audible at a great distance and why a neighbor's stereo will keep you awake at night.

Dense material blocks some sound. Stiff, rigid materials deflect some high pitched sounds while conducting other lower pitched ones. Concrete might muffle a good percentage of noise, but steel, for example, actually conducts sound waves more efficiently than air. Noise moves into a home by way of any openings, no matter how small. Old, shrunken weather stripping around windows and doors will let sound waves in. Other kinds of openings, like vents for clothes dryers, mail slots, and pet doors, provide easy access for all wavelengths.

There are many cost-effective noise blockers that reduce exterior racket. Seal openings with silicone bulb-type weather stripping. Look for gaps between baseboard and floorboard, exterior doors, and windows. Then check the fireplace. Is the flue shut? Also, keeping windows closed significantly reduces rumble. Fresh air can be quietly funneled through an HVAC (heating, ventilation, air-conditioning) system. Seal off or remove pet doors and mail slots. Add glass storm doors to reduce traffic and neighborhood noise.

Block and break up sound waves that enter through roof vents and clothes dryer vents by adding a length of tubing that curves into an S shape. An offset curve breaks up the wave. It is hard for a wave to bend around several tight curves, thus making it more difficult to enter the house.

More ways to block outside noise involve more cost. Fencing out noise can stop it dead in its tracks. Make sure fencing is dense and tall (anywhere from six to twelve feet). Concrete, concrete blocks, brick, or overlapping wood panels are effective materials. Fences add privacy and security, but they call for an investment, particularly if they enclose an entire property line. It is possible to use fences only where the most noise emanates. Check local codes before embarking on a fence project. Most codes do not allow fences close to the street and require a fence to be set back anywhere from six to ten feet. Planting evergreens and privet hedges also helps to muffle noise.

Building an addition to the house is another solution. An addition can absorb racket if it is positioned to block the source, or it can be placed out of the way of bothersome noise to create a quiet sanctuary.

If you are planning an addition to buffer the bluster, use few or no openings for the most sound blocking. Even if the addition is relatively narrow, additional living space will be welcome. For insulation, use cellulose, fiberglass, or rock wool, all of which are superior to rigid foam for sound dampening. Anywhere from four to six inches of insulated dead space is sufficient.

Another option is the addition of a glassed-in sunporch that extends one or two stories. It will not only add space and visual appeal but will intercept unwanted sounds. Glass, of course, is not as dense as concrete, but it will cut down some noise. Special glass such as thermopane and other kinds of double-paned glass that feature an air space work best. A sound-blocking sunporch does a nifty job of keeping the peace while providing a brilliant space for year-round indoor plants.

Form a quiet zone by placing an addition at the opposite side of the house from the problem. Plan on using that space for rooms that call for peace and quiet: bedrooms, a home office, or entertainment areas. Using denser materials, good insulation, and positioning windows away from potential noise sources ensure tranquillity.

A Word about Windows

A perfectly designed window for acoustical purposes has a four-inch air space between panes and an insulated frame of vinyl or aluminum that prevents the transmission of noise and loss of energy. This type of window is not available in stock. It must be custom made. Stock standard double- or triple-pane windows are considerably less expensive. Consider replacing older single-pane windows in your home with the insulated, double-pane type to lower noise levels and reduce heating and cooling bills. For more information, refer to chapter six.

Doors

Two doors are better than one. Install a year-round glass storm door to deaden noise. The difference in sound level will be immediately apparent. Furthermore, glass storm doors are reasonably priced and easy to install. Most home improvement stores carry several choices that feature beveled effects, stained glass insets, and more.

Exterior doors should be single-panel solid wood for best noise control. The runners-up are insulated metal or fiberglass. If your grand entry door has sidelights and a transom, a very handsome and inviting look, make certain the glass is double-paned.

Effective exterior noise baffling brings down interior sound levels by five decibels or more. Although the number sounds small, it is significant: forty-five decibels is comfortable, fifty decibels is not. Every effort made to reduce noise will increase the ease and convenience of your home.

Interior Solutions

Most interior clamor comes from appliances. Machines make noise. The noisiest, most machine-filled place in the house is the kitchen; dishwashers, trash compactors, ice crushers, blenders, can openers, garbage disposals, ventilators, and refrigerator compressors all add to the din. Many are in operation simultaneously. When harsh sounds from these power-driven appliances bounce off hard surfaces and reverberate, noise is intensified. Add to that all the other sources of airborne noise, which include running water, rattling dishes, clanging pots, television, and chatter. Impact noise, such as footfalls, travels through surfaces and adds to the ruckus.

A hushed home is easy to achieve. Mechanical engineers explain that to reduce noise levels, you must identify the three parts of the sound problem: the *source*, the *path*, and the *receiver*. As the receiver, you could wear earmuffs to suppress unpleasant sounds, but there are more efficient methods to block the path of bluster and quell din at its source.

Several steps can be undertaken to muffle sound at its source and decrease the opportunity for airborne and impact noise to make a path to you. The following strategies are relatively inexpensive.

- If you are building a new house or relocating an existing kitchen, plan to place it as far as possible from noise-sensitive areas, such as your study or bedroom.
- If you are knocking out walls and redoing space for a great room, create short-angled walls that deflect sound.

- Enclose your kitchen. Use solid-core doors equipped with soft rubber or plastic gaskets. If light is peeking around gaskets, sound is also leaking through. Use weather stripping around doors.
- Make your own sound-rated doors using Acoustilead (a thick lead sheet sold in rolls of four feet by twenty-five feet for about $2 per foot).
- Build in some soundproofing with behind-the-scenes sound blocking and sound absorbing materials that turn walls, floors, and ceilings into effective sound barriers (more about materials later on in this chapter).
- Create sound barrier partitions by using a double-wall construction technique that involves staggering two-by-four studs that break up the path of sound as it travels. Soundproofing insulation batting is then wound between the studs to absorb sound. Sound-deflecting acoustical planes are nailed to the studs and covered with wallboard. Experts say you can lower sound volume by about four decibels in this way. A three-decibel difference is audibly noticeable.
- Add noise-absorbing acoustical materials to the surface of walls, floor, and ceiling and inside cabinets and countertops.
- Select quiet appliances and install them properly to avoid annoying vibrations.

About Sound Ratings

To muffle nerve-jangling racket, both sound absorption and sound isolation are necessary. Materials carry two kinds of ratings, STC and NRC. *Sound Transmission Class* (STC) rates the effectiveness of material as a sound insulator. The higher the STC rating, the better the barrier will stop sound. Most interior walls have STC ratings between 30 and 35, which means that loud speech is still audible from room to room. *Noise Reduction Coefficient* (NRC) indicates the absorbency of the material. The higher the NRC rating, the more sound absorbent the material. In certain situations, you will need to consider both ratings before choosing the best material.

To build in extra sound barriers, install an acoustical wood fiber board behind the drywall, floors, and ceilings. Some materials are suitable for all three areas, and only installation techniques may change. Georgia-Pacific's Hushboard fiberboard panel can be applied in wall construction to create partitions with STC ratings of 46 to 50, which means that loud speech is barely audible. Hushboard is also recommended for ceilings. Sound Deadening Board, another Georgia-Pacific product, is designed to resist sound transmission through walls and floors. An STC rating of 50 can also be achieved by nailing Sound-A-Sote by Homasote to both sides of a conventional sixteen-inch stud wall, countersinking nails one-sixteenth inch below the surface, staggering panel joints from side to side, and laminating the acoustical paneling made of recycled newsprint with five-eighths-inch wallboard.

For quieter floors, Homasote's Comfort-Base can be laid over a concrete slab. Because it has a half-inch-thick panel that is kerfed with a stress-relieving four-inch by four-inch grid on one side, carpet and pad can be laid directly over Comfort-Base. Add a wood underlayment if you decide to use a hard-surfaced flooring like ceramic tile or wood parquet or a soft surface like vinyl tile or sheet goods. Created especially for apartment buildings, this is an effective tactic in single-family residences where quiet is a must.

AKZO's Enkasonic (a pliable mat composite of nylon filaments and nonwoven fabric) can be sandwiched between the subflooring and a support overlay. For example, it's effective when installed between floors and under hard surfaces such as ceramic tile and stone or a carpet and pad, where both the STC rating (measuring airborne noise) and ratings measuring impact noise must be above 50. Enkasonic matting was used in the homes of director Steven Spielberg and actor Arnold Schwartzenegger who both have at-home sound studios. Enkasonic matting retails for about $2 to $3 per square foot ($27 per square yard) making it one of the more expensive solutions.

For sound-blocking materials in walls, floors, and ceilings to be most effective, all openings must be sealed. A hairline crack will increase a partition's transmissions by about six decibels, so use an acoustical caulk for all seams and fill in any holes or gaps to block the sound path.

Decorative Solutions

In addition to home improvement projects, consider decorative solutions. Surface quietness can be enhanced by using soft materials and fabrics for wall, floor, and ceiling surfaces to soak up sound. If you have ever walked through an empty house, you know firsthand how much finishings soak up reverberations. Some materials and finishes are better choices than others for getting the job done.

Wall coverings will absorb more kitchen noise than hard surfaces, such as ceramic tile, wood, or paint. Washable vinyl wall coverings are a practical choice. A new alternative for lounge areas of kitchen and great rooms are fabric-covered acoustical panels. One example is Homasote's Design Wall, a recycled fiberboard interior panel with an NRC of 0.20. Design Wall is available in a variety of standard and custom colors.

While in-floor materials block sound, soft surfaced floor coverings absorb it. Carpet absorbs ten times more airborne noise than any other flooring material and as much as most other types of standard acoustical materials. For example, the NRC for carpet laid over a forty-ounce hair pad over concrete is 0.55 versus a rating of .05 for wood parquet on concrete. Carpeting virtually eliminates floor impact noises, and it is a highly efficient thermal insulator. This, plus the fact that it can be laid directly over inexpensive subflooring, makes it a real value.

Kitchen carpeting, a staple of the '60s and '70s, is reemerging as a flooring choice of the '90s. Kitchen carpeting is a lightweight, flat, continuous-filament, low-loop pile that won't hide food crumbs. Usually, kitchen carpeting bears a four-color pattern design, a jute or foam backing, a stain-resistant coating, and carries a wear warranty. The price ranges from $10 to $16 a square yard. An abundance of colors and sophisticated patterns are now available, making it suitable floor covering for adjoining family and dining rooms.

Another choice for a quiet floor cover in an open kitchen is vinyl, which has an NRC of 0.05 versus 0.000 for terrazzo or stone. Seventy-three percent of all vinyl flooring is installed in the kitchen, where its soft foam backing helps to muffle impact noise. Cleanability is a strong advantage, too.

More Silent Treatments

Sound bounces off ceilings, so it is wise to look for materials that will give a room the silent treatment. Washable acoustical tile in a no-grid look, and interesting patterns and designer colors make it a stylish and functional choice throughout the house. Acoustical tiles are available in three types of materials: mineral fiber, wood fiber, and fiberglass. Mineral fiber and fiberglass are fire retardant and meet Class A requirements for certain building codes and fire regulations. Wood fiber ceilings are designed for use where combustibility is not a factor. Sound ratings depend on material and construction, so you must check the ratings marked on the carton. Pick one with an NRC of 0.65 or 0.75 that will really reduce noise levels.

Weigh NRC and STC ratings when choosing a ceiling for a room with specific noise reduction requirements—a nursery over a media room, for example. NRC measures the amount of sound the interior finish will soak up. STC measures how much of the sound will go through the ceiling to the room above or below. Simply looking at an NRC rating will not give you the whole picture. If the material has a high NRC and low STC, sound may be absorbed within the room but will transmit straight through to the next floor. Fiberglass is such a material. In this case, a more appropriate choice would be a denser material made from wood or mineral fiber that has a relatively low NRC, but a higher STC that would cut down on noise passing through the ceiling.

Acoustical tile ceilings should be suspended from the ceiling for best results. The thicker the air space between walls, floor, and ceiling, the more effective noise reduction is. Air is the least efficient conductor of sound. Three to four inches of air space works best and would allow for a backload of dropped or suspended panels of additional insulation. Insulation materials include cellulose, rock wool, and fiberglass. The millions of tiny pockets resist the flow of heat and cold. Rock wool is similar to fiberglass except that it is spun from rocklike materials. Cellulose is made from recycled newspapers. Fiberglass comes in easy-to-handle precut batts and rolls. Both can be used inside walls and ceilings to absorb sound.

Acoustical wood and mineral-fiber ceilings can be painted with latex flat wall paint. Fiberglass ceiling panels are flexible and should not be painted. An acoustical ceiling for a typical kitchen costs between $50 and $200 depending on whether it is washable and fire-retardant.

New Earth-Friendly Appliances and Technology

Nonpolluting and environmentally safe appliances are popular with consumers. Appliance manufacturers have responded by designing earth-friendly appliances that generate less pollution and far less noise. According to market research, noise abatement is a priority for manufacturers, along with energy efficiency and designing products that can be recycled.

Engineering noise out of appliances is achieved through installing sound-dampening materials in the cabinets that house dishwashers and washing machines. These materials consist of two metal skins with a sound-dampening core sandwiched between. Bearings systems installed underneath a washer or dishwasher can also cut down vibrational noise.

For specifics on noise emission, check the decibel rating of the appliance and ask for a demonstration before you make your purchase. Dishwasher manufacturers tout quiet features. Among them are more foil-covered fiberglass insulation in more places (especially doors), asphalt-based sound dampening sheets on tops and sides of tubes, sound-deadening gaskets, polystyrene sound barrier shells, and rubber ring mounts to isolate the motor and pump and absorb vibrations. If you would like to retrofit a dishwasher with noise-reducing insulation, contact the manufacturer. Some companies offer additional insulation material as a service part you can order and install.

Stove and oven ventilation systems are essential for removing smoke, odors, and excess water vapor. The National Bureau of Standards advises choosing a squirrel-cage type ventilator over noisier fan types.

Build in your own sound barrier by lining the dishwasher, refrigerator, and trash compactor cabinet cavities with sound-absorbing materials such as Armstrong's Sound Soak. Flexible plastic and rubber hoses minimize vibrations that are transferred to the floor and walls. Place

Common Sound Intensity Levels in Decibels

110 Accelerating motorcycle
100 Auto horn
 90 Kitchen blender, orchestra
 70 Average radio
 60 Average office
 50 Average conversation
 40 Quiet home
 30 Quiet conversation
 20 Whisper
 10 Soundproofed room
  0 Threshold of hearing

QUIET!

45

large and small appliances on rubber mats or pads to dampen the din. Use wooden cabinets, which are quieter than plastic laminate, and line shelves with cork tile. Install solid-surface sinks (they are quieter than stainless steel). Add draperies, upholstery, and area rugs and your kitchen will be serene.

Inside the home, natural and artificial lighting serves both practical and aesthetic functions. An effective lighting scheme illuminates, boosts productivity, heightens convenience, improves safety, establishes mood, directs traffic flow, and highlights precious objects. Creating the perfect lighting plan means taking into account such details as room size, windows, and exposure.

Many homes, however, are built without much thought given to lighting. Too little light, poor distribution, or faulty color temperature causes eyestrain and headache. Something bothers us when we encounter bad lighting—the nebulous but very valid "It doesn't look good." There is no excuse for bad lighting. Improving the lighting scheme in your house is one of the easiest and most affordable home improvement projects you can undertake.

Light Facts

As part of an overall effort to reduce electricity consumption and reduce electrically generated pollution, Congress passed the National Energy Policy Act (EPACT) in 1992, which outlaws inefficient lightbulbs and other energy wasters. Some states, like California, even dictate that energy-efficient fluorescent bulbs must be the primary lighting sources in kitchens and baths. Meanwhile, new technology has made it possible for manufacturers to make smarter, more efficient, longer-lasting lightbulbs with improved color-rendering abilities.

Using the new bulbs will mean savings in energy consumption in the long run, which also means lower electricity bills. Lighting accounts for 15 percent of a typical household's electric bill. Switching to a more efficient mode of lighting will mean savings over the long haul. Replacing a single incandescent bulb with a fluorescent bulb could mean that 500 pounds of coal will not have to be burned.

The biggest change has been in the area of fluorescents. New technology has made it possible to produce fluorescents that better mimic natural sunlight. Fluorescent lighting is now available in a range of cool and warm color temperatures making it possible to pick the best one for any environment. Fluorescents, once strictly available in long tubes or circles, now come in a variety of shapes and sizes that allow them to be

CHAPTER 5

Comfortable Lighting

used as replacement bulbs for almost any light fixture. New dimmer switch technology for fluorescents allows for some variation in light levels, a plus for home application.

Since April 1995, all lightbulb packaging must display, by law, the output of light per watt (called lumens per watt or LPW) and the color rendering index (CRI). The LPW and CRI information will allow you to purchase lightbulbs that best meet your needs and your budget.

The LPW will tell you which bulbs are the most efficient sources of illumination, allowing you to comparison shop for energy savings. Watts tell us how much power is consumed, but not how much light is produced. Thanks to new technology, lightbulbs are more efficient at producing light. No longer is there a strict correlation between how much power a bulb is using and how much light it's producing.

To make finding the right light bulb easier, the color rendering index is supplied on the packaging. The closer the CRI is to 100, the more it resembles natural sunlight. A CRI in an acceptable range (80 and up) guarantees that your colors will stay true and your skin tone will look youthful. Artificial lighting strives to emulate the white light of the sun's rays, which is actually composed of the visible spectrum of color from red to violet. It is vital to check the CRI of a fluorescent, since a light that is too cool emits only short, cool wavelengths of light and fewer longer, warmer wavelengths. Improvements in fluorescent technology enable these bulbs to emit warmer, sunnier light.

Light is talked about in terms of color temperature and is measured in degrees kelvin. Color temperature is a scientific way to describe light. Have you noticed how different sunlight looks on a rainy afternoon compared to a sunny afternoon? You probably have also observed how sunlight differs from season to season. The change in relative positions of the sun and earth creates changes in the color temperature of the sunlight. As a result we respond to this shift in color temperature by adjusting the colors in our wardrobes seasonally. In the summer, we respond to the intense sunlight by wearing lighter colors. We wear deeper colors in the winter to compensate for the "cooler" natural light.

How a color looks under a given light, from sunlight to candlelight to halogen light, is known as *color rendering*. What makes any particular object a certain color is its ability to absorb all the other wavelengths and reflect only a specific wavelength to the viewer. Looking at the color rendering index is a faster way of knowing how the light will behave and a little easier to grasp than the more abstract notion of color temperature.

More Light Facts

The study of light is called optics, from the Greek word optikos, which means sight. Light consists of the visible wavelengths of electromagnetic radiation. Red lights have the longest wavelengths, violet the shortest. The farther away a light is, the dimmer it appears to be.

Objects reflect light. The amount of reflection varies according to the value of the object's color, which in turn dictates how much light will be needed in a given room. The lighter the colors in a room are, the more they will reflect light, whether it is from the sun or a man-made source. The same room decorated in darker values will call for significantly more light.

White, the palest color, returns 80 percent of the light striking its surface. Black, however, absorbs 95 percent of incidental illumination and returns only 5 percent. Therefore, if a bathroom, for example, is remodeled from a pale pink (a light value) to hunter green (a dark value), more light is needed simply to maintain the previous level of perceived illumination.

Texture also plays a role in the lighting selection process. The more texture, the more light required. Wallpaper calls for extra lumens. The opposite, of course, holds true. The less texture, the less light required. The optimal surface is a matte finish that reflects light evenly and reduces the need for illumination. The size of the room, the number and position of windows, and the kinds of furnishings (large, dark pieces soak up light) must be factored in during the information-gathering stage of light planning.

Lighting Your Life

Lighting controls the flow of people, indicating where activities are to take place. Good lighting is seamless. People see a room and then see its important details. Bad lighting is obvious. Dark shadows, hot spots, and harsh glare all make a room uncomfortable and ugly.

Good lighting is the result of a smart plan. To devise a lighting strategy, measure the room dimensions and chart information on your floor plan (for more information on how to make a floor plan, see chapter seven). Include windows, doors, and furniture placement. Jot down any relevant information about activities and special needs. Make several copies of your room grid to explore different possibilities.

Take all this information to the lighting store. The more information you have, the faster you can sift through the huge assortment of lighting options. You may also want more help than a salesperson may be able to provide. If so, arrange a professional lighting consultation with a certified lighting consultant who can be recommended by a representative from your local American Lighting Association (ALA) showroom. To find the showroom nearest you, check the Yellow Pages under lighting consultants and designers, or telephone the ALA at 800/274-4484.

Lighting is an affordable means of improving the home. Additional electric wiring might be called for, however, since many older homes are inadequately wired, have few outlets, and switches are poorly positioned. Talk with your electrician about estimates and recommendations.

If you are designing or refurbishing a house, plan for adequate outlets and switches. How many you need and where they should be located will depend on furniture placement and room function. If a room has too few outlets, plugging in lamps and other electric appliances might be impossible or simply dangerous. Long cords running around a room are unsightly and contribute to accidents. According to experts, frayed electric cords are still a common cause of fire and electric shocks.

When you finish devising your lighting strategy, you will also want to run cost estimates on your plans. Price fixtures, receptacles, switches, and all hardware. Ask for bids from three licensed electricians. Plan on doing all hardwiring and complicated behind-the-walls work first. Calling an electrician back several times to make changes can be expensive.

Design is a solution to a problem. Your problem is to safely, effectively, and beautifully illuminate a room so that it functions conveniently and harmoniously. Lighting design is broken down into three kinds of illumination: general lighting, task lighting, and accent lighting.

General Lighting

Also referred to as ambient lighting, general lighting functions like sunlight to illuminate an entire space. The main goals of general lighting are visibility and safety. Ambient light bounces off walls and ceilings to cover as much area as possible. Light-colored ceilings and walls with matte, glare-free finishes reflect the most light and make the room appear larger.

The fixtures that deliver ambient or general light are up lights and down lights. Use a combination of both to illuminate your rooms. Up lights, such as torchères and wall lamps, are designed to aim illumination toward the ceiling and provide indirect light to a room or hallway. Pendants, table lamps, and floor lamps radiate light toward the ceiling and floor. Recessed lights in ceilings or concealed behind cornices, valences, or wall brackets cast radiance down.

Task Lighting

Task lighting is illumination for small areas. This kind of lighting should be bright enough to accomplish tasks, but must also be balanced with the surrounding area. The general or ambient lighting should be at least one-third as bright as a task light. An overly bright work lamp cannot compensate for a dimly lit room. Eyestrain will result. Correct any deficiencies in general lighting by using higher LPW bulbs in fixtures or increasing the number of fixtures. Good fixture choices for task lighting are well-positioned recessed lights, track lighting, pendants, table or floor lamps, and under-cabinet lighting strips. Focused light beams should minimize eyestrain and allow for detail resolution. Position your work light carefully to avoid glare and shadow.

Accent Light

Accent light spotlights an object. Use a bulb that is no more than three times as bright as the surrounding ambient light (the ambient light should be one-third or more as bright as the accent light). Position the fixture to prevent the light from interfering with the line of sight and to avoid reflections on other surfaces. Accent lights can be successfully used to illuminate art on walls or objects on table surfaces. If you have objects or details of special importance, you will want to introduce accent lights where appropriate, but use restraint and good judgment. If every single object is highlighted, the objects lose their importance and the eye will be confused.

Lighting Balance

Your first step is planning the ambient lighting. All other lighting will be brought into balance with it. For example, if one end of the room has plenty of sunshine, you will need to add an equal amount of light at the other end. Structure your lighting plan with an effective combination of bright, medium, and muted light. Vary the amount and intensity of light according to how the room is used. Kitchens and baths need the most light. The media room, for example, requires a lower level of overall lumens. Bedrooms need sufficient levels to aid dressing, ease eyestrain if much reading is done in the room, and imitate natural sunlight, especially in the morning and during winter months. Light is what stimulates the human body, so you will want to have adequate amounts to get you going.

Think also in terms of the entire house and plan room by room. As you move through the house, there should be no dark places or inaccessible light controls. This is a crucial safety factor. Position light control panels so that it is possible to turn on lights as you move into a new area.

Entryway lighting might simply consist of some up lights that cast indirect light. Accent light might highlight displays of art. Hall closets should have interior lights and interiors should be painted light colors to reflect light. Hallways throughout the home should be adequately lit. For safety, the hallway light should be a happy medium between the most softly lit and brightest rooms in the house, so that moving from a darkened (or bright) room into the hallway is not hard on the eyes.

In bathrooms, think about safety. Fixtures and bulbs must not interfere with splashing water or wet hands. The shower light should be a wet-location recessed fixture or surface-mounted wet-location fixture that will help prevent shock. If using fixtures above the shower, make certain they are sealed against moisture. Shower proof fixtures are designated by manufacturers by specially marked packaging. Mirrors help to bounce light around a room. For making up and grooming, use shadow-free lights around the mirror.

In a bedroom shared by a couple, plan for separate task light areas for reading with separate controls so one can read while the other watches TV or sleeps. Light the interior of closets to make early morning dressing easier. General light need not be overly bright, as task lights and accent lights do more of the lighting work where required. Window treatments should let in adequate amounts of daylight as needed.

In young children's bedrooms, remember to protect them from shock, heat, and being alone in the dark. Place controls at a low level and use dimmer switches, night lights, and reading lamps. Use individual lamps with independent switches for bunk beds. Take extra precautions with wires, making sure that lamp cords are neat and out of traffic flow.

Safely light stairways. Avoid flat light. Use a strong directional light at the foot of stairs to increase contrast between risers and treads. At the top of the stairwell, use a down light. Controls should be at the foot and head of stairs. Strip lights can also be placed at each riser for twenty-four-hour illumination. Of course, all stairs should have handrails. Concealing lighting at the handrail is another way to keep stairs safe.

Control

Planning how to control light is crucial in the well-designed home. You should never be in the dark nor backtrack to turn off and on lights, nor should you have to get up out of bed to turn on or off the lights. The most basic types of light control involve wall switches. The simplest is the single pole. If a room has more than one door, install a three-way switch (a switch at each door) or a four-way switch (conveniently positioned to control lights from three or four locations). There are several kinds of wall switches: on-off toggle, rocker, slide, and touch-sensitive switches are the most common. For children, older people, or the physically challenged, chose a touch or slide control switch. Most are available in illuminated models. Face plates come in lots of styles and price ranges, but usually whatever matches the wall surface is the best choice.

Dimmers for key lights are a must. They reduce the flow of current, and that in turn adjusts the level of illumination from soft and romantic to bright and energetic. Dimmers reduce electric consumption and increase the life of bulbs. Incandescent dimmers are inexpensive and dimmer switch kits are easy to install yourself.

The best kind of control now available is an *integrated dimming system*. Various kinds of lights—general, task, and accent—are wired to computerized circuitry. The integrated dimming system is a sophisticated piece of equipment and a must for complex lighting systems. The touchpad calls only for slight touch, and the system can be preset to create multiple preset lighting systems within each room which are called *scenes*. The living room, for example, might have several lighting scenes: bright general light and task lights for reading at night, low-level lighting for quiet conversation, or softer ambient light and accent lights for entertaining. Each scene can be recalled by touch of a predetermined button from a single wall control box or hand-held wireless remote control.

Other control options involve sensors that turn on the lights as soon as someone enters a room. Infrared control and sound and motion control sensors seem to work almost magically, turning on the lights as soon as they sense the presence of a moving or warm body. These sensors are convenient—you never need to remember to turn a light off or on. They will also conserve electricity, since lights are turned off when no one is there. You may want to make sure that this kind of automatic switch has a manual override, since some lights turn off automatically if there has been no motion in the room for awhile. It's possible to be sitting quietly and reading and have the light go off right in the middle of the most exciting passage.

Light and Shadow

The contrast of light and shadow is the key to understanding how to light a room. The eye needs time to adjust when moving from a light area to a dark zone. It takes about five minutes for the eye to adjust adequately. Therefore, think in terms of keeping light consistent or plan transitional stages to reduce shock. On the other hand, a reasonable amount of contrast is desirable. Differing levels of light let the eye rest as it moves from bright to dark. Contrast also creates visual interest and mood. Plan for two or three areas of stronger light to generate a focal point in a room.

Glare results where there is too much contrast. If light is reflected from an object and strikes one spot, it is called a hot spot. Direct glare from a bare lightbulb is ugly and dangerous; replace it with a coated bulb or put a shade over it. Veiled glare occurs when a fixture is placed above a flat, glossy horizontal surface and the light bounces up. Reflected glare results from an interaction of a light source and a vertical plane. Because glare causes the eye to cope with two levels of light simultaneously, it causes eyestrain and headaches.

Avoid daylight glare through open windows. The extreme contrast stuns the eye. Use shades on windows and match the brightness throughout the room. Window walls—walls that are mostly windows—in kitchens often call for more, not less lighting in an effort to create a balanced lighting scheme. At night, lights reflect off the panes and cause glare. Place lights away from windows and use window treatments for glare elimination and privacy.

Track Lighting for Accent Light

For lighting objects on walls or lighting the wall itself, position the track and the fixtures at a thirty-degree angle. Generally, fixtures should be aimed at this angle to prevent hot spots and glare. Allot one fixture per object. Wall washing for nontextured surfaces adds interest and illuminates artwork. If ceilings are nine feet high, mount the track two to three feet from the point where wall and ceiling meet. For ceiling heights between nine and eleven feet, place the track lighting four feet away from the wall. Space fixtures equidistantly. Wall grazing creates dramatic shadows on textured walls and surfaces. Mount the track closer to the wall than for wall washing, using a distance of six to twelve inches and aiming the lights downward. Wall grazing enhances brick, stone, and even an extraordinary drapery. If enough track lights are used, the spill effect may be enough to provide general illumination.

Recessed Lighting for General Lighting

You can use a number of different types of lightbulbs in recessed lighting fixtures, including general service (A) bulbs, reflector (R), parabolic reflector (PAR), or ellipsoidal reflector (ER). A bulbs cast light over a broad area, R bulbs cast a broader beam, and PAR and ER bulbs cast focused beams of light. To find out how many fixtures you will need for any given area, consult the manufacturer's literature. Darker colored rooms will need more wattage and LPW than rooms with light color schemes. Also, ALA showroom experts can help you determine how many lights you need, what types of lightbulbs to use, and where to place them in the room.

Light Solutions for Dimming Vision

Vision impairment begins generally around age forty, when suddenly everyone needs reading eyeglasses. Not only do aging eyes generally need eyeglasses, but as one ages, more light is needed for any type of close work. For reading, a middle-aged person needs twice as much light as a twenty year old, and a seventy-year-old person needs three times as much light as a twenty year old for reading and other specific tasks. That light should be glare-free, since as one becomes older, eyes become more sensitive. The American Lighting Association (ALA) offers the following suggestions:

- Provide general lighting throughout the house in sufficient quantities for balanced, glare-free illumination. Recessed down lights are the best bet. There are new halogen bulbs that fit regular household sockets and are suitable for down lighting. Augment down lights with wall sconces, cove lighting, and floor lamps.
- For reading, use an adjustable halogen task lamp. The halogen bulb produces more light per watt than a regular incandescent bulb, so you'll get extra brightness without boosting your light bill and it will last longer than an incandescent bulb.
- Under kitchen cabinets, install slim fluorescent or low-voltage accent lights, which will make reading recipes easier. Mount these energy-efficient fixtures near the front of the cabinet. In the bath, mount a lighted magnifying mirror with a swing arm on the wall next to the vanity for shaving and applying makeup.

COLOR EFFECTS OF INTERIOR LIGHTING

Type of Bulb	Color of Light Emitted	Brightens	Mutes
Incandescent	yellowish white	warm colors	cool colors
Fluorescent			
Cool White	bluish white	green, yellow, blue	red
Warm White	light amber	red to yellow, skin	red, blue
Cool White Deluxe	white	virtually all	none
Warm White Deluxe	white	red orange	blue, green

The Shapes and Forms of Lighting

Hall/Entry Fixtures

These produce general lighting for safety and a congenial atmosphere. Use ceiling, chain-hung, or close-to-ceiling fixtures in hallways, stairways, and entryways.

Pendants

Pendant lights provide task or general lighting and are suspended from the ceiling over a table or work area. Small halogen pendants can be used over end and night tables when space is at a premium. Use a dimmer for flexible lighting. Pendants come in a wide variety of styles.

Chandeliers

This special type of pendant is based on the idea of the candle. Flame-shaped lights come in incandescent or halogen varieties. Use a dimmer for varied light intensity and a romantic effect.

The following tips are suggested ways to trim consumption to save the environment and reduce your electric bill.

- Turn lights off when they are not needed.
- Install infrared or sound and motion control switches that automatically turn lights off when the room is not in use.
- Install dimmers to lower light level and electrical usage.
- Use timers or photoelectric cells for outdoor lights.
- Use more efficient reflector bulbs for task and accent lighting. Substituting a fifty-watt R for a one hundred-watt A uses half the electricity and provides the same level of light.
- Replace incandescents with energy-efficient fluorescents. Yearly savings on electricity range from $40 to $126.

Ceiling Fixtures

Ceiling fixtures deliver general light and are practical for illuminating any space. Incandescent, halogen, and compact fluorescent models are available.

Wall-Mounted Fixtures

These furnish general, task, or accent lighting and come in a variety of designs that will match and supplement other forms of lighting. Incandescent, halogen, and compact fluorescent models are available.

Bath/Vanity Lighting Strips

Task lighting for grooming is provided by these gently glowing incandescent globes. They create a professional Hollywood makeup studio look and are effective for makeup application.

Portable Lamps

These include any light that is designed to be movable, such as torchères, table, floor, and clamp-on lights. These supply general, task, or accent lights. Upright cans, minireflector spotlights, desk, and piano lights provide only accent or task lighting. Incandescent, halogen, and compact fluorescent models are available.

Track Lighting

Track lights furnish general, task, or accent lighting all at one time and are flexible. Lights can be moved, swiveled, rotated, and aimed at individual points along the track. Pendants and chandeliers can also be hung from the track. Incandescent, halogen, and compact fluorescent models are available.

Recessed Lighting

Recessed lights provide general, task, or accent lighting inconspicuously; only the trim shows at the surface and the actual light is set into the ceiling, which is ideal for low-ceiling areas. These are available as down lights, adjustable accent lights, wall washers, and in incandescent, halogen, and compact fluorescent versions.

Undercabinet/Undershelf Fixtures

These fixtures offer task and accent lighting. They are great for under kitchen cabinets to light the countertop or work area and are also good for curio cabinets, bookshelves, or any other spot that needs a highlight. You can get them in fluorescent, miniature track, and strips of low-voltage minilights.

Light Living Tips for Living and Family Rooms

- If your room features stone and brick walls or fireplaces, use recessed lights to bring out the texture of the brick.
- Add interest to long walls and hallways by creating a scalloped effect of light with wall washers.
- Place reading lamps behind the reader's shoulder, forty to forty-two inches above the floor. Use a shade that ends at eye level to avoid glare.
- Highlight paintings with halogen track lighting.
- Accent houseplants with an up light, which can placed between the wall and the plant to create a dramatic silhouette.
- Center halogen pendants over bars and counters.

Light Living Tips for the Dining Room

- Suspend pendant lighting thirty inches above the tabletop and use a fixture that is twelve inches narrower than the tabletop.
- Use a chandelier as a focal point in a dining room, hanging it thirty inches above the tabletop and allowing six inches of clearance on each side.
- Position a ring of four track lights or recessed halogen lights over a table to make table settings sparkle.
- Accent a buffet by situating wall sconces on either side and placing recessed lights twenty-four to thirty-six inches apart above it.
- Install strips of halogen minilights under the shelves in a hutch or china cabinet to highlight your china and collectibles.
- Put a soft focus on artwork with recessed adjustable fixtures or halogen track lights.

Light Living Tips for the Kitchen

- General lighting from overhead, energy-efficient fluorescent tubes supply diffuse light. For kitchens with lots of natural light, the fluorescent lighting should be as bright as sunlight in areas that are far away from windows.
- At the sink and range, install compact fluorescents for individual, recessed down lights as task lighting.
- Islands also need task lighting; suspend pendant lighting thirty inches above the surface.
- Undercabinet lighting is a must. Mount fluorescent strips (twelve to forty-eight inches long) close to the front edge of cabinetry to avoid glare. Lighting should cover two-thirds the length of the counter.
- Kitchen cabinets that have glass panes benefit from low-voltage minilights over, under, or inside cabinets.
- Place additional strips of tiny incandescent lights in soffits and other concealed locations to highlight cabinetry and add a warm atmosphere to the kitchen.

Light Living Tips for the Bedroom

- Dimmers are a must for bedrooms.
- Use ceiling fixtures, fan lights, recessed down lights, or wall sconces to provide sufficient general lighting for dressing and seeing into closets.
- Install recessed or surface-mounted lights in closets. Energy-efficient fluorescent strips or compact tubes are great alternatives to incandescent lights.
- Use table lamps or strips of light for vanity areas.
- For reading at night, use table lamps positioned to prevent glare and eyestrain.
- If space is at a premium, use recessed lights or pendant lights.

- Swivel-arm wall lamps are classics. Use one on each side of the bed.

Light Living Tips for Children's Bedrooms

- Track lights are versatile and safe sources of light for task and accent lighting.
- Place controls no higher than thirty inches from the floor.
- Use easy-to-operate rocker or slide controls.
- Guard against your child being alone in the dark. Install lightbulbs with a built-in backup filament.
- Use smart lightbulbs in lamps. These lightbulbs have programmable microchips that gradually dim the bulb over a period of time or that shut themselves off.
- Keep a wall-mounted flashlight for emergencies.
- Provide a night-light with built-in sensor that turns on when light levels are low. Place these in hallways and bathrooms as well.

Light Living Tips for the Bathroom

- For added heat, install an infrared heat lamp.
- Small bathrooms may only need up lights positioned over a mirror or strip lights around a mirror.
- Mount decorative wall brackets at both sides of the mirror. Add one at the top if additional light is needed. Wall brackets should be sixty inches off the floor.
- Use warm white fluorescents for energy-efficient lighting.
- Install theatrical globe lights around the mirror.
- Larger bathrooms may require ceiling fixtures. Use warm white fluorescent or incandescent bulbs.
- Tub and shower enclosures need an enclosed damp location recessed down light in the ceiling.
- Use enclosed damp location recessed down lights over whirlpools and saunas for added safety.

Light Living Tips for the Home Office

- Think of glare-free lighting strategies. Eliminate harsh contrast.
- Place two or more large, energy-efficient fluorescents to the fore and aft of the desk area for well-diffused general lighting that eliminates shadows.
- Credenzas should be illuminated with undercabinet lighting. Use fluorescents and place them close to the front of the cabinet to prevent glare.
- Use accent lighting to create pleasing areas in the office.
- Position adjustable portable lamps to the side and rear of computer screens to reduce glare.

Windows have incredible powers. An amazing array of designs help us distinguish cottage from castle and a host of architectural styles in between. Architect Ileana Martin-Novoa calls windows "magic." She and her husband and partner, architect Jonathan Katz, AIA, often use windows to perform magical feats. They transform ugly-duckling houses into swans that are as beautiful on the inside as they are on the outside. For example, they used 125 custom windows and twenty-five skylights to give a typical Dutch Colonial house a more classic eighteenth-century facade. Inside, formerly cavelike rooms were suddenly opened to floor-to-ceiling views of a beautiful garden once seen only from the out-of-doors. One hundred twenty-five windows may seem extravagant, but there is not one extraneous window in this wonderful design.

Ileana and Jon used a few, much less expensive stock windows to give a typical suburban ranch house a more dignified Colonial character. Despite the difference in the number and the cost of these windows and those in the Dutch Colonial *cum* Classic house, the results were the same. That is, there was an amazing change in the appearance of the house. In the twinkling of an eye, the owners were given the greatest of gifts: front-row seats at nature's glorious color show, the changing of the seasons.

New windows should look and perform beautifully. We want a window for all seasons and expect a window that closes tightly against Arctic blasts to open effortlessly to summer's balmy breezes. Thanks to space-age technology, windows do both these things. They also come in a vast array of styles, shapes, and sizes.

The key to beautiful, comfortable windows is to pick the right window for the right job. To do this, Ileana and Jon suggest a nine-step approach.

1. Determine the extent of work to be done.
2. Decide which window type and size relates best to the style of your house.
3. Study orientation to views and solar exposure.
4. Consider your need for openness versus privacy.

CHAPTER 6

Window Magic: Comforting Windows and Window Treatments

5. Imagine the placement of windows on a wall as viewed from outside and inside.
6. Think about window placement in relationship to decor.
7. Investigate materials (ranging from vinyl, vinyl clad, aluminum, wood, and so forth).
8. Keep energy efficiency in mind.
9. Compare costs.

The ninth step—comparing costs—is the tricky one. It's apt to encourage you to change your mind from a very expensive (but divine) custom window to a similar (but never exactly the same) stock or standard window that's kinder to your budget. Sometimes, the trade-off is not too painful; at other times, it can be heartbreaking.

When you analyze what new windows can do to make your house more comfortable, the project may be less intimidating than you think. Perhaps it's only one window that's troubling. For example, you may be risking back injury every time you reach across your kitchen sink to raise a stubborn double-hung window. Replacing it with an easy-to-crank-open casement will eliminate the risk. Maybe you need to get from the dining room to the patio. A sensible solution is to exchange the double-hung dining room windows for French doors. Do you need fresh air in your living room? Then replace that old '50s picture window, which is actually a fixed pane, with a row of elegant casement windows. Add elegance and admit more fresh air with a row of awning windows (these crank open from the bottom outward) below the casements.

Changes such as these do not require major remodeling efforts, nor do they have to cost a lot. If you are changing one or more windows to update performance or looks, choose replacement windows—they're the kind that fit into existing sashes. You'll have to match and patch existing siding, but you will save money and time since you don't have to tear out and replace the sash. Total renovation (removing siding and tearing out walls) gives you a lot more flexibility; you can place new windows of radically different sizes and shapes in the facade. In many cases, total renovation has given rise to whole walls of windows. The Pella Company calls combining windows of various sizes and shapes into one particular design *windowscaping*, a trend that's transforming cavelike rooms into garden rooms all through the house.

Windowscaping is easy to do. Just combine various basic window types and shapes that have been around for a long time. The two most common are double-hung and casement windows. Double-hung windows stack top and bottom sashes that move up and down to open for ventilation. The traditional version features true divided lights; that is, small panes of glass separated by wooden muntins. Contemporary versions have one large pane of glass with a removable grille that makes cleaning easier.

Casement windows are hinged on the left or right and crank outward. Large vertical panes give them a modern look. Adding diamond-patterned grilles gives casements a cottage style. Often, these windows are hung in pairs. Once-popular jalousie windows with their hinged horizontal panels are drafty and not much seen today. Instead, windows that allow for an uninterrupted view of nature are used, and various opening options are available.

Awning windows can be used alone or in combinations with casements for effective ventilation and good looks. If wall space is a priority, awning windows placed high on the wall leave the wall free for furniture. This arrangement also offers greater security, since they're more difficult to reach. Of course, all windows should have secure locking devices.

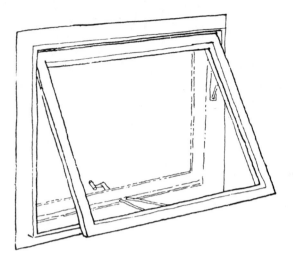

Casements: Sashes crank open from the sides or center

Circlehead: A half-round window that usually does not open

Double-hungs: Stacked windows open by sliding up or down past each other

Fixed frame: Immovable window

Oriel: Similar to bay, but extends halfway to floor

Today, windows are available in more standard or stock sizes than ever before. Additionally, most major manufacturers make windows in custom sizes and shapes. You dream it, and some manufacturer can surely make it. This means that you can replicate a unique antique window with one that looks exactly like it but has double or triple insulated glazing that makes for a warmer room.

The fact is, new window technology encourages exciting walls of windows regardless of geography. Unlike the old single panes of glass that did little to keep out cold or heat, new low-E (low emissivity) glass is coated so that it reflects radiant heat rather than allowing it to pass through the glass. Windows engineered for northern climates reflect heat inward, keeping it inside the room. Windows made for use in warm southern states reflect the heat outward so that interiors remain cooler.

The insulating quality, or R value, of a window is increased when air in the space between double and triple panes of glass is removed and replaced with argon or some other heavier-than-air gas.

Tinted glass contains chemicals that absorb light and heat radiation, which reduces glare and brightness. The shading coefficient of this glass varies from about 50 to 70 percent. Some tinted glass with special UV coatings offer protection from the harmful effects of ultraviolet rays. Several companies make a coated sheet of tinted, translucent material that professionals can apply to a window in a few hours.

These innovations cost a little more initially, but they conserve energy and make it possible for you to sit by your window comfortably any time of the year. However, builders in southern states who commonly use single-pane glass say that most heat loss and gain is through the roof, so more insulation in the ceiling is what really matters. They reduce their building costs by installing single-pane windows. But homeowners wind up paying higher energy bills and cover windows that they can't sit near on a hot day.

Sitting beside a single-pane window on a hot summer day in the South is just as miserable as sitting in front of one on a cold winter's day in the North. Homeowners in cold climates tend to expect and get high-performance windows, like those that architects Katz and Novoa used to surround a wood-burning fireplace in a New Jersey great room

Illustration opposite:
High-performance windowscaping around a fireplace in a New Jersey home allows in light but blocks the heat and cold.

where their clients enjoy the comforts of both a crackling fire and a beautiful winter garden snowscape.

WINDOW INNOVATIONS

- **Clear insulating glass windows:** designed with an air pocket between panes for better insulating
- **Argon-filled low-E** (low-emissivity) windows: filled with inert argon gas for insulation and coated with metal oxide to reflect heat in summer, absorb heat during winter
- **Argon-filled double-coated low-E** windows: block damaging sun ultraviolet rays
- **Single levers:** simple, effective locking devices for casement windows
- **Double-glazing panel system:** a removable second pane of glass that allows addition of blinds, pleated shades, or removable windowpane dividers; has thirteen-sixteenths inch of air between panes for energy performance and to reduce outside noise transmission
- **Casement** windows: with energy-efficient insulating glass with look of narrow windowpane dividers; choose a casement sash that opens toward the center for easy cleaning
- **Rolling screen:** rolls up and out of sight for an unobscured view (provides 40 percent more light than conventional fixed screen)
- **Aluminum exterior** window frames: clad with baked enamel coating that does not require painting
- **Removable grilles:** make a single large pane look charming; cleaning is easy
- **Outside mount sliding door panel:** sliding glass door featuring weather stripping that actually becomes tighter when the wind blows
- **Tempered glass:** manufactured at an extreme temperature and cooled rapidly to prevent shattering when broken

Window Treatments

Bare windows may be beautiful, but sunlight-bright wakeup calls, unrelenting glare, and heat buildup can be unpleasant and unwelcome. Light can be marvelous, but there are times when it must be controlled. Some windows are available with built-in blinds, but for those that aren't there are many options, including venetian blinds, miniblinds, vertical blinds, wooden shutters with movable louvers, old-fashioned roller shades, and new accordion shades that combine a light-filtering sheer with an opaque mate. Graber makes a metallicized shade that's treated to filter the sun's rays. All of these window treatments will make your room more comfortable, but each blocks or alters light flow in a different way, which may determine a particular choice for a particular room. For example, louvered wooden shutters are great choices for almost any interior. Traditional, narrow-vaned shutters are especially suited to traditional interiors. Shutters with wide vanes, sometimes called plantation shutters, are more contemporary looking. Installing shutters in top and bottom rows offers great flexibility and maximum comfort. For instance, the bottom row can remained closed at all times for privacy while the top half is opened for maximum sunlight and views. Louvers on individual panels operate separately for customized light control. No other type of window covering works in quite the same versatile way.

An old-fashioned window shade, installed so that it pulls up from the bottom, can be lowered all the way for maximum light and view, pulled halfway up for privacy over the lower half of the window, or pulled to the top of the window for maximum blackout and privacy. Shades do not offer the advantage of a shutter's movable louvers that can be partially opened for a light-dimming effect.

Venetian blinds or the newer miniblinds can be lowered part or all the way and offer a light-dimming effect with vanes that can be partially opened. Shutters, which combine independently operating narrow panels, offer still greater flexibility. Often, the deciding factor is style preference.

Draperies and curtains, long ignored in favor of bare windows, are making a comeback. Unlike purely decorative lengths of fabric or swags and jabot, lined draw draperies and curtains block out unwanted light and outdoor noise, and they absorb indoor sound. Lined Roman and balloon shades, which can be drawn up into attractive folds and poufs when you're ready to let the sun shine in, are also light and sound barriers. Consider combining shutters, blinds, or shades with draperies or curtains for the greatest and most flexible light and noise control.

All these window treatments help block drafts and keep in heat. In addition, they provide excellent opportunities to bring the aesthetic comforts of color, line, pattern, and texture into your rooms. If you need decorating advice in making these choices, it's readily available free from a wide variety of sources, starting with decorating magazines and books. Specialty drapery shops and workrooms offer advice, and furniture and department stores offer inexpensive, helpful interior design services.

Floor plans reflect the mechanics of your lifestyle. The term *floor plan* refers both to how the space inside a home is laid out, room by room, and how furnishings are arranged within the room. This chapter deals with both these meanings, first discussing the major issue of the way interior space is utilized, and secondly, touching upon the general theory involved in planning a room.

A well-conceived layout follows the logic of how you live. The goal of a good floor plan is to make your home a machine for living, to make your house serve you instead of forcing you to work hard to serve your house.

Unfortunately, most houses are laid out badly. Bad traffic flow turns every room into a hallway. Poorly placed doors and windows steal precious wall space. Noisy rooms situated next to quiet ones rob people of solitude. Thoughtlessly placed entrances waste our time and energy with extra steps. Wasted space that could be used for just about anything forces us to live only in a fraction of the house. Our style is cramped. A lack of grace notes—no entryways, inadequate entertaining space—spoils the home.

Floor plans that serve you reflect the logic of modern living. When a house functions perfectly, the mechanics of living feel effortless. Well-planned space seems luxurious. To establish step-saving space, add grace notes, and redefine interior areas, you should rethink your house's layout from the viewpoint of comfort and convenience. The customized layout accommodates individual needs. These layouts are tailored for entertaining, working at home, leisure pursuits, gourmet cooking, studying, tending to young children or teenagers, and other special demands.

The idea of customizing or altering the plan of a house may seem like a luxury or indulgence, but custom floor plans are a necessity for convenient living, not an extravagance reserved for only few deep-pocketed souls. A layout that solves problems will make the house more functional and will add to its value.

Making better use of space means applying basic design intelligence. Floor plans in new houses are designed to be more accommodating to contemporary living styles. Builders are continually trying new concepts in space configuration. An evolution in layout has optimized space, making it more flexible.

CHAPTER 7

Creating Comfortable Floor Plans

What are some modernized features? Volume (high ceilings, double-storied rooms, lofts, balconies) has replaced cost-effective eight-foot ceilings. An open plan has preempted separate, compartmentalized rooms. Kitchens have merged with dining and family spaces to form great rooms, taking us full circle to the place where everything started, the one-room house. Master bathroom suites (some houses boast two) have evolved into multifunctional exercise/spa and dressing areas.

An emerging trend is the reinvention of transition space between outdoors and indoors. For the last few decades, home layouts have neglected the entry area. Perhaps to allocate space elsewhere, perhaps due to a decline in at-home entertaining, homes have been designed with no buffer zone. Residents and guests alike crossed the threshold and walked directly into the private sphere of the home. You open the door and you are in the living room—no mystery, no surprise, no set-aside place to check your appearance or leave the trappings of the outside.

To the ancient Greeks and Japanese, the outside belongs outside. Home is a temple. One needs to shed the outer garments to come into the sanctuary of home. To the Greeks, one was a hero on the battlefield, but entered the home a mortal. The Japanese view is that the outside world and inside world are opposed; to bring the outside to the inside defiles the home spiritually. The entryway is at the border of the interior world where one exchanges walking shoes for cozy slippers. There are some practical benefits to such spiritual credos. The house stays cleaner, the floors last longer, and thermal energy is preserved.

Floor Plans Through the Ages

The floor plan has evolved over the centuries from one room to highly specialized rooms to open living. In late-eighteenth-century American homes, a classical emphasis on the symmetrically balanced, rectangular shape replaced the less functional asymmetrical style. Fireplaces were centralized for energy efficiency. Downstairs floors had two rooms in the front half, two in the back, and a central staircase. With this plan, traffic could flow conveniently, and householders could find privacy.

Post-Revolutionary America established its own architectural voice. American architect Asher Benjamin's *The American Builder's Companion* declared American cultural independence from European style and called for a new sense of architectural egalitarianism. New World materials, a new taste for a cleaner look, and a need to economize on labor and materials called for a purely American approach to home design. The goal was clear: to bring *comfort*, dignity, and quality to all classes.

As the economy and technology improved, so did house plans. The Federal floor plan placed the hallway and stairs to one side. This plan has remained popular and is still used in townhouses today. The Federal plan makes the most of limited and narrow spaces. It also keeps public and private spaces neatly separated and retains the separateness of each room. Typically, one must pass in and out of the room through one door. Some homes feature a pocket door that slides so that living and dining rooms may be conjoined.

The next leap forward in floor planning came as reaction to the precision of classicism. Victorian, Gothic Revival, Italian villa, and Romanesque styles freed architecture from the notion that houses and rooms had to be rectangles. These new designs featured rooms that were anything but square: circular, octagonal, and irregularly shaped rooms were the trend. Although these various approaches were stylistically different, they did share one common design element: floor plans reflected a sense of isolation; each room was a small box (whatever its shape) that served one purpose only and was cordoned off from the rest of the house by doors. Rooms had no visible connection to each other. The result was that rooms felt remote and disconnected.

The turn of the century ushered in a whole new take on building and decoration that reflected the expressive and utilitarian qualities of new building techniques and materials. A new design philosophy was born that would take into account the form and function of architecture and furnishings. Frank Lloyd Wright was the first to free the home of rigidly defined, boxy rooms with his revolutionary *space blocks* that formed the basic units of the house. Japanese homes had traditionally been constructed using an open plan. Wright adapted the Eastern concept for the Western home. The space blocks were open areas for living and dining that implied, rather than designated, the purpose of the space. The L-shaped living/dining room is an example of how space blocks were adapted by builders and architects for home construction.

Wright's Prairie Houses, built around the Chicago area, blended the home into the surrounding landscape and integrated the principles of cubism to create a convenient and holistic environment. Wright extended his architecture into the house, creating built-in furniture—everything from closets to sofas. Inspired by Wright, American technology, and Cubism, European architect Le Corbusier framed the concept of the home as a machine for living. As a machine facilitates a function, so should design.

For a good example of how the home has evolved along the lines of Le Corbusier's machine for living, take the humble closet. Surprisingly, it took thousands of years for people to dream up the simple convenience of integrated storage space. First, simple and small storage areas replaced chifforobes and armoires. It was not until after World War II that the average American home even had closets. Shallow, narrow, inadequate closets of the first half of the twentieth century presaged the more functional walk-in closet of the second half. Now, walk-in his-and-her closets placed near the master bath form a bath/dressing area. Grooming is faster. Dressing is easier and more private.

Designing Your Floor Plan

An essential element of the well-designed floor plan is the idea of home as shelter, room as sanctuary. The house itself is a refuge. Each room maintains a feeling of asylum, separating the outside from the inside, the public from private, the earthly from the heavenly. Usually, most houses separate communal and private space. The foyer or entry hall serves as a buffer, a transitional area, between the spheres. The more public living and dining rooms are kept separate from private, personal bed/bath areas through dividing the house into sections or wings. Mundane functions (such as eating and bathing) require separate spaces from those designated for spiritual activities, such as reading, listening to music, conversing, and studying.

For a room to be a room, there must be a feeling that a particular expanse is set apart and special. You can achieve this by creating effective seating arrangements—a sofa flanked by two chairs, for example. Traffic flow, however, must be routed away from conversation groups and activities. Conversation or other pursuits can then unfold in a more intimate setting without interruptions.

A workable, intelligent layout must meet your needs, not hypothetical requirements. Many builders' floor plans meet the needs of the client in a marginal way. Some floor plans are useless. A builder's criteria for design, however, is not the same as the architect's. Builders' floor plans must take into account cost control, ease of construction, and the general taste of the market. Contemporary homes may or may not meet your demands or your older home may need updating to make the best use of space.

To achieve the best floor plan for your lifestyle, you must examine your needs and your preferences. Would your house benefit from knocking down walls and putting up new ones? Would an addition solve all your living problems? Would furniture groupings be more satisfying if doors and traffic paths were altered?

Achieving the most comfortable arrangement of space may be a simple matter of drawing up plans with a good carpenter. Changing the location and size of a closet or moving a door can be done relatively quickly and at a reasonable cost. It may not require too much effort to make substantial living improvements. If the solutions are relatively simple—moving a door, or even walls—then a carpenter can execute your plan.

If you have ample but unlivable space and you don't quite know how to maximize it, consult an architect. The architect is only as good as the information that you, the homeowner, give to him or her. To give information, the homeowner has to sit down and think about the personal needs of family members. An architect can suggest a number of solutions that will fit into your budget.

Think of ease and convenience if you plan on doing remodeling. Take note of which tasks are hindered by the layout of your house. Correcting the flaws of an inconvenient layout will make life easier. Kitchens with easy access to the garage make it easier to carry in groceries, for example. Decks that allow passage into the kitchen enhance entertaining. Home offices situated in quiet areas allow for concentration. Bedrooms placed away from family rooms permit one family member to rest while others play.

Get to know your needs before you build or remodel. The following checklist is a quick way to gather information about the requirements of your lifestyle. The information will allow you to determine what you want from your house. You can zero in on specific areas that need immediate attention. Address other needs later as your schedule and budget allows. Also, you might discover that you don't need to totally redo your house. A few essential changes might be all you need to make your home functional.

The Custom Floor Plan Checklist

How would you describe your personal style? (Check one.)
- ❏ Casual and easygoing
- ❏ Refined and sophisticated but comfortable

Do other householders have the same preferences? Are they willing to compromise?
- ❏ Yes
- ❏ No

What type of room plan do you prefer?
- ❏ Open plan
- ❏ Traditional rooms

What type of community is your house in?
- ❏ City
- ❏ Country
- ❏ Residential (suburb)

How often do you entertain small groups (one to four)?
- ❏ For barbecue/buffet_____ times a month
- ❏ For dinner_____ times a month
- ❏ For dessert/coffee, drinks_____ times a month
- ❏ For football games, TV, video_____ times a month
- ❏ For conversation_____ times a month

How often do you entertain larger groups (four or more)?
- ❏ For barbecue, football games_____ times a month

❑ For dinner _____ times a month
❑ For dessert/coffee, drinks _____ times a month
❑ For football games, TV, video _____ times a month
❑ For conversation _____ times a month

How many times do you hold family reunions and other big parties?
❑ _____ times a year

What age ranges do you and other family members entertain?
❑ Families with children
❑ Young children
❑ Teenagers
❑ College age
❑ Adults
❑ Older people

How often do you have weekend guests? How many? _____
❑ Less than two to four times a year
❑ More than four times a year

Which rooms does your family gather in?
❑ Kitchen
❑ Living room
❑ Family room
❑ Other _____

Rank the functions of your home.
❑ Basic shelter
❑ Elegant living
❑ Entertaining
❑ Work
❑ Hobby
❑ Family development
❑ Weekends/vacation
❑ Personal pursuits and activities

What rooms do you need?
❑ Entry
❑ Family room
❑ Home theater
❑ Music room
❑ Master bedroom suite

❑ Bed/bath suites_____
❑ Guest room_____
❑ Living room
❑ Bathrooms—how many?_____
❑ Dining room
❑ Breakfast room
❑ Kitchen
❑ Utility room
❑ Hobby room
❑ Home office
❑ Study
❑ Other_____

Check the amenities you need.
❑ Security system
❑ Built-in bookshelves
❑ Wet bar
❑ Indoor pool
❑ Live-in help
❑ Intercom
❑ Stereo/TV system
❑ Fireplace
❑ Other_____

Check architectural elements desired.
❑ Deck
❑ Patio
❑ Porches
❑ Balconies
❑ Skylights
❑ Atrium
❑ Dormers
❑ Courtyard
❑ Arches
❑ Other_____

Preparing a Floor Plan for Furniture Arrangement

Drawing a floor plan isn't brain surgery. Thanks to graph paper (choose the one-fourth inch equals one foot scale), you can easily and inexpensively rough out a floor plan. You may not even need a ruler.

First, measure the length of each wall. Then, allowing one square for each foot, draw lines that represent each wall on your graph paper. Measure the widths of windows and doorways, and note how far they are from the end of the wall. Mark them on your graph. A rectangle represents a window. Erase the line to indicate the doorspace, and draw a line that indicates which way the door swings. Once you've drawn your room (or whole house) on graph paper, make several photocopies so that you can easily experiment with colored pen or pencil on revisions—moving doors and windows, expanding the length or width of the room and so on—until you find a plan that suits you.

Use the following checklist to help you sketch the features of your room. Record measurements where necessary.

- ❑ Where are doors?
- ❑ What direction do they open?
- ❑ Where are windows?
- ❑ Where are air-conditioning and heating vents located?
- ❑ Where are thermostats?
- ❑ Where are light/electrical switches?
- ❑ Where are electrical outlets?
- ❑ Where are light fixtures?
- ❑ On ceiling?
- ❑ On wall?

Measure:*
- ❑ Distance from floor to ceiling
- ❑ Length of each wall_____

Doorways: width_____ height_____
- ❑ Door: width____ height____ frame width, projection____
  Open door takes up how much wall space?_____

*Overall length and width measurements should be taken at floor level. Add together all distances between features (from each door to window). The measurements should be close.

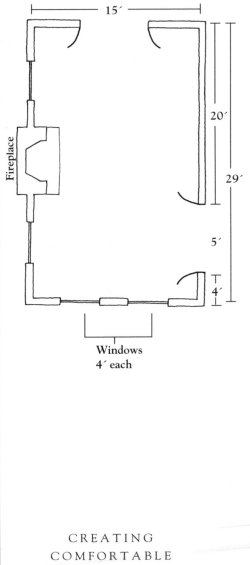

Windows
4´ each

CREATING
COMFORTABLE
FLOOR PLANS

81

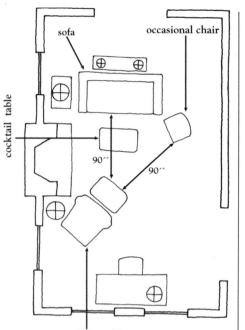

sofa

occasional chair

cocktail table

90'' 90''

easy chair and footrest

Windows: from floor _____ width _____ height _____
☐ Glass: width _____ height _____

Floor Planning Area Requirements for Furniture and Traffic Flow

Guidelines for Furniture Placement in Conversational Groupings

Once you've got a rough floor plan, planning a furniture layout is equally as easy. There's no need to draw your furniture in place. Instead, use inexpensive, scaled furniture templates available in stationery and crafts shops. The one-fourth inch equals one foot scale templates will correspond to your graph paper. Some furniture manufacturers and retail stores also provide templates in their catalogs and brochures. Occasionally, decorating magazines publish tear-out templates. These templates, which are made of paper or cardboard, can be easily pushed around your graph floor plan until you find an arrangement that suits you.

If you're not sure how much space you should leave between various pieces of furniture, refer to the following guidelines. These guidelines are helpful, since we tend not to leave enough room for easy passage. And, in real life, furniture looks closer than it does on a floor plan because of the height and bulk of upholstery and closed cabinets. These rough spatial comparisons are adequate for determining comfortable arrangements for most rooms.

Measure both footprint (outside dimension, how much floor and air space a piece will actually occupy) and actual usage space for best results.

- The average person probably needs about twenty-four inches of seating space. The typical American's hips need about fifteen inches to eighteen inches for ease of movement. Additional inches are needed for knee-crossing and arm movement and for personal psychological space. Optimal seating distance between speakers should be a minimum of twenty-four inches to a maximum of ninety-six inches, measured from speaker to speaker.
- *Couches, sofas, divans:* Seat height should be fifteen to sixteen inches from the floor (down-filled cushions may be higher but compress upon use). Back-to-front footprint measurements range

from narrow seats at twenty-eight inches to overstuffed seats at forty inches. Length ranges from a small sofa at sixty-six inches, which only seats two, to an *average of seventy-two inches to eighty-four inches for three,* to ninety-six inches long, which seats four.

- *Love seat or two-seater:* Seat height should be fifteen inches to sixteen inches from the floor. Length ranges from forty-two inches to sixty-three inches.
- *Recliners* need a minimum footprint of thirty-two inches by seventy-nine inches for a fully extended position. Tall people (five feet ten inches and over) need models with a three-inch higher back and four inches of additional leg space.
- *Easy chairs and club chairs* require a minimum footprint of thirty-two inches by thirty-two inches to sixty-six inches. Seat height should be fifteen inches to sixteen inches, width from thirty inches to thirty-eight inches, and measure front to back from twenty-eight inches to thirty-eight inches.
- *Side chairs and occasional chairs:* For extension of elbows and legs, allow twenty-eight inches by thirty-six inches. Seat height is seventeen inches, width is twenty-four inches to twenty-nine inches, and front-to-back measurements range from twenty-four inches to twenty-eight inches.
- *Folding chairs* should have a footprint of eighteen inches to twenty inches and a width and length of twenty to twenty-two inches. Seat height should be sixteen to seventeen inches.
- *Stools* should have a seat height of fourteen to sixteen inches, and measure thirteen to eighteen inches in circumference.
- *Benches:* Seat height is fourteen to sixteen inches, width is thirteen to eighteen inches, and length is eighteen inches or more.
- *Service tables* for coffee, cocktails, or snacks: Allow for a minimum of thirteen inches between the seating unit and the table for knee space. A sofa and a table with knee space takes up ninety-three inches of total floor space. Heights range from fourteen inches (too low) to twenty inches (high). For easy reach, a coffee table should be slightly higher than the seat.
- *Television viewing:* The center of the screen should be thirty-two to thirty-eight inches from the floor if viewers will be sitting,

reclining, or lying in bed. If suspended from the ceiling, a television must hang lower than pendant lights.

- *Stereo systems:* Elevate speakers from the floor according to the manufacturer's suggestion. Speaker sizes vary from mini to enormous. If buying a stereo, take your floor plan to the electronics store for advice on what is best for the room's size.

Measurements for Dining Areas

- First determine how many guests the room will accommodate. Take the square footage of the room and divide by fourteen square feet to calculate average spacing. A ten foot by twelve foot room (120 square feet) divided by fourteen square feet means enough space for eight guests, including table, chairs, and serving aisles. If the room has several doors and storage cabinets, fewer guests can be accommodated.
- *Dining table space:* Allow a minimum of twenty-four to twenty-six inches per table setting. Round tables with pedestals are the most efficient for seating and space. Oval tables, corners, and table legs take up to eighteen inches of unusable space. Table heights should be twenty-nine inches to thirty inches from the floor.
- *Chair seating space:* Armchairs should be twenty to twenty-six inches wide by twenty to twenty-six inches deep; optimal seat height is eighteen inches from the floor. Side chairs should be eighteen to twenty-four inches wide by twenty to twenty-six inches, with a seat height of eighteen inches. Allow twelve to eighteen inches of space for a seated diner and the chair. Allow eighteen to twenty-four inches from the edge of the table for rising from the chair.
- *Serving aisles:* Allow an additional eighteen inches to pass by seated diners. From table to wall, a minimum of thirty-six inches is needed; if meals are served to guests, allow forty-two inches to the wall.
- *Consoles for storage and serving:* Minimum width should be sixteen inches for chargers or dinner plates. For serving, the best height

from the floor is thirty-two to thirty-nine inches. A minimum height of eighteen inches is needed for handling coffeepots, platters, and soup tureens. Allow an eighteen-inch aisle space, twenty-four inches for work space, and thirty to thirty-six inches for opening cabinets and drawers.

Measurements for Bedrooms

- A mattress should be a minimum of three inches longer than the person who sleeps on it. Twin mattresses are thirty-nine inches by seventy-five inches, extra-long twins are thirty-eight inches by eighty inches; doubles are fifty-four inches by seventy-five inches; queens are sixty inches by eighty inches; kings are seventy-six to seventy-eight inches by eighty inches; California kings are seventy-two inches by eighty-four inches.
- Extra long mattresses are seventy-eight to eighty inches long. These are usually custom made.
- For figuring how much space your mattress will occupy, add three inches to the width and length for bed coverings. Add three to four inches to the length for the thickness of the headboard, and another three to four inches for the footboard.
- For two beds, allow a minimum of twenty-four inches between beds (include bedcover width).
- Place a chest of drawers where there is a minimum of thirty inches of extra space to open drawers easily.
- For sofa beds, allow a minimum of eighty-four inches of space for opening; allow eighteen inches of surrounding space for general usage.
- The width of a mattress plus box springs measures fifteen to sixteen inches. Standard distance from floor to top of mattress measures twenty to twenty-two inches.
- Measure all bedroom doors to make sure the mattress can be moved into the room.

For information on measurements for kitchens and bathrooms, consult chapters ten and twelve.

Inn days long past, the living room was the front parlor, seldom visited and almost never enjoyed. Daily family life took place in the kitchen, around the kitchen table, fireplace, or stove. The well-appointed parlor was saved for important company and formal occasions.

Those of us with a choice between using the living room or den may not have progressed far enough from the notion of living room as a place *just for company*. Lately, we've seen a rash of rooms furnished wall to wall with white carpeting, white sofas, glass-topped tables, and glitzy mirrored walls. No one ever uses these rooms. Who are they for? Surely not the neighbors; they have their own. Perhaps these living rooms are not actually intended for living, but it's hard to see the point of a *for-show* room, while family living is relegated to a den, family room, kitchen, or great room somewhere in the rear of the house. What a waste!

Of course, some of us have no den, only a single living room, but with today's technological advances in stain-proof fabrics, wipe-clean floorings, and easy-care furniture, it's no longer impractical to live in our living rooms. To make the most out of a living room, think in terms of function and comfort.

Not everyone, we admit, wants a usable living room. We have seen at least one living room that functions strictly as an art gallery. Take our young, single friend whose thirty-foot-plus living room holds five objects. At the end of one wall, there's a black iron shelf that displays several art objects. Against another wall is a large glass-front display case. An oversized oval table displays a gigantic art vase. There's one side chair—also an *objet d'art*. That's all. She loves it. Arriving guests marvel, then they all move on to the den.

If the rest of us agree that living rooms are for living and that the sofa won't be ruined if someone sits on it, what next? What will make the living room a comfortable space?

Entry

First, establish a sense of transition from the street. None of us wants to open the front door and march directly into the living room. Certainly we don't want strangers doing that. If there's no entry hall, replete

CHAPTER 8

The Living Room

❧

with coat closet, bench for pulling off boots, and a powder room or at least a mirror for a quick primp, then we need a screen. There must be some sort of shield between the door and the rest of the room. All too many houses have monster doors, eight feet high or more, that open directly and abruptly into living rooms that look like hotel lobbies because there are no walls, only doorways. There's no sense of destination, only passage. Who could be comfortable in a hallway? We want to feel secure in a room.

Comfortable Furniture Groupings

What attracts us to casual living areas is the sense of ease. Whether your style is sophisticated or casual, let those same feelings of barefoot, blue-jeaned comfort be present in the living room. There should be an absence of ostentation and intimidating decoration. Every effort should be made to make the room comfortable and functional. A living room should have at least one place for sitting and conversing, reading, or taking a glance at the evening newspaper, as well as serving refreshments. If your home has a living room but no den or family room, the living room must also accommodate many more functions. These include watching television, taking a nap, playing games, working on needlework or other hobbies, and countless other messy things. We need to engage in these activities without fear of recrimination. Children aren't the only ones who spill a drink or drop a plate of food.

Granted, common sense suggests that some activities (all right, the messier arts and crafts ones) should be relegated to the kitchen or basement. More social ones—sharing the newspaper or a TV show, games, hobbies, and so forth—can be enjoyed in the living room. Clearly, a key to comfort is finding furniture and furnishings appropriate for the activities planned for that room. The logical first step in creating a supremely comfortable living room begins by listing the activities you'll be doing in that room, matching the furniture to the activities, and deciding where in the room to place everything.

A living room is most commonly used as a gathering place for people to sit and talk. How many family members will be using the room on a regular basis? How many guests will you have? How many people will gather? How big should your sofa be? How many chairs will you need? Where can they be placed? How much or little distance should there be between chairs for conversation and for uninterrupted traffic flow? Refer to the guidelines for furniture placement featured in chapter seven.

Conversation groupings should include seating arrangements with an appropriate amount of space between people. Never put two chairs so near each other that people are too close for comfort. The friendlier and more intimate the relationship, the closer two people will be. Generally, only lovers wish to be closer than two feet apart. Others converse comfortably at a distance of three to four feet. No one can talk normally if they're more than eight feet apart. If you're in doubt as to whether your chairs are too close or too far from one another, watch your guests at your next gathering. They'll adjust their own chairs to suit themselves.

Each seating arrangement should include a table or a surface for serving refreshments. Balancing a drink in one hand and appetizers in another while trying to shake hands can be embarrassing for guests. We recommend having tables at several heights for both convenience and visual interest.

Remember that you should arrange your living room with its purpose in mind. If you enjoy reading, you'll need a bookcase. If you like listening to music and watching television, you'll want to plan the best possible seating to enhance enjoyment. You might also want to store media equipment in a handsome media cabinet so that when it is not in use, it is also out of sight. Likewise, if you play cards, you'll need a card table. Where will you place it? Will your living room space allow for a permanent game table, or will you need a folding table? Should a permanent table be placed by the window (you'll play in the daytime), or should your delicate lady's desk go there?

The larger the room, the more furniture it will hold, and the more difficult these decisions will be. The best ploy for dealing with the large room is to treat it as though it were several small ones, made up of various seating and activity areas.

Every room needs a focal point. This is one of those design rules that always works. An important piece of furniture such as a sofa (we've never seen a living room without one) is a natural focal point. One way out of the "where do I start" maze is to determine where the sofa, generally the largest piece in the room, will go. Keep in mind that a sofa should almost never be placed directly in front of a window. Do so *only* when the view is disappointing or if the room gives you no other choice. In almost any room, there's a stretch of wall uninterrupted by windows where the sofa seems at home. You could flank the sofa with two well-stuffed occasional chairs and add a rectagular or square coffee table, end tables, and handsome lamps. Hang interesting art above the sofa. This gives your room a strong focal point, a classically comfortable furniture arrangement, and the beginnings of a welcoming room.

Another convention is to place the sofa and an end table at one side of the fireplace and two lounge chairs with an end table between on the opposite side. A tall bookcase or television placed against the wall opposite the fireplace adds balance and is accessible to all within the room. Nearby, two chairs and a corner lamp table create a reading nook. To the other side of the bookcase, a small writing desk and side chair fill the corner. Other pieces of furniture (a radio in a cabinet, a low chest) occupy the walls to either side of the fireplace. In a fifteen-by twenty-three-foot room, there's ample space for all these pieces and for moving around them. The room provides for multiple activities with no sense of crowding.

Planning a room even this simple is best done on graph paper. Sketch your floor plan to scale. Put major pieces in their most logical places, then doodle until you've worked out a satisfactory arrangement for the whole room. Don't hesitate to experiment. It costs nothing to erase and redraw your lines, and that's much easier than moving furniture. There are times, however, when graph paper doesn't show all the relationships between furniture and architectural features. Sometimes, moving furniture is the only sure way.

Don't be shy about shedding certain notions. As mentioned, generally a sofa should never go in front of a window. That's a good maxim. But a living room in a New York City brownstone proved an exception. The sofa was placed in every conceivable spot with no success. Each time we put the sofa in a new spot and stepped back to view the results, we met with dismal failure. The room still looked uncomfortable. Finally, in desperation, we placed the sofa in front of tall French windows. Voilà! What a great look. It was difficult not to run and dive headlong into its great, plump cushions. The delighted homeowner, Elizabeth Bianco, a former decorating editor for *Redbook* magazine, was thrilled with the results. Experimentation made it happen.

When you're placing your furniture on graph paper, leave ample space for traffic. Most of us need at least two feet between objects. Leave four feet for aisles. If space allotted for traffic patterns leaves no room for particular pieces of furniture, don't panic. There's probably something that you can use successfully instead. For example, if a lamp table takes up too much room, consider a floor lamp with a smaller glass shelf. Surprisingly, even the best of us sometimes overlook the obvious solutions.

There are a number of floor plans today that are especially difficult to deal with. One is the L-shaped room. Some try to create a sense of two distinct rooms by using a piece of furniture as though it were a wall at the juncture of the two rooms. Using a buffet to separate the dining ell from the living ell is one such strategy. We do not advise breaking up the space in this way. It seems more satisfactory to treat the two areas as one.

Small living rooms with several doorways are another headache in the making. All too many of us have furniture pushed against the walls, leaving traffic with nowhere to go except right through the middle of the room, traversing the only conversation area. Depending on where doors are placed, it is better to move furniture groupings closer into the room and leave a clear passageway behind them. This theory might make some people nervous because free-and-clear walls are unorthodox. We seldom see a wall without at least one piece of furniture against it. However, we guarantee that no wall is going to fall simply because there's no furniture nearby.

When the Layout Says Remodel

Occasionally, it's necessary to take one more drastic step to correct the faulty architecture that created an awkward room by moving one or more doors. A cousin's house in Indiana is a case in point. Her living room entry is catercorner from the door into the kitchen, creating a

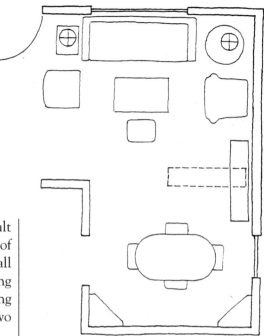

Treating the L-shaped room as one continuously flowing space.

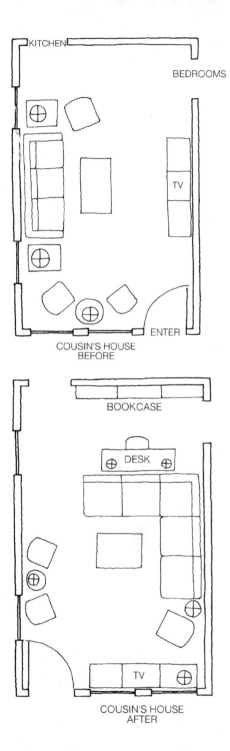

COUSIN'S HOUSE
BEFORE

COUSIN'S HOUSE
AFTER

strong diagonal traffic pattern that cuts off conversation and a view of the television. On one side wall there's a door into the hallway leading to the bedrooms. This creates a second diagonal walkway that makes the living room about as calm as a waiting room at Grand Central Station. A simple and inexpensive solution would be to move the front door in line with the door to the kitchen. This would create a straight walkway between the two. A modular sofa on the wall near the door to the bedrooms would create a sense of continued passage. The television could occupy the corner where the entry door had been. Then, those sitting on the sofa would have a clear, uninterrupted view of the screen. Perhaps the next time we're there, we'll sketch out my suggested floor plan.

Built-Ins

You may consider building in some of your furniture. Whether you do or not is a matter of personal taste and preference. But, should you yearn for change, you can't take it with you, nor can you move it to another spot in the house.

Consider the Architecture

Architectural elements, including built-in furniture, fireplaces, niches and nooks, windows and doors, and bookcases all create a mood that must be considered along with furniture layout. The theoretical layout of a floor plan on graph paper doesn't show how furniture will relate visually to the architectural elements in a room. That fact helps explain why the sofa in the New York City brownstone finally found a home. At one end of the long, narrow room there was a fireplace. At the opposite end were floor-to-ceiling cabinets and bookshelves. Behind the sofa was a wall of French windows. Opposite the sofa was a row of arched openings similar to those in a loggia. It's no wonder the sofa looked embraced and sheltered in front of the windows.

Selecting Furniture

There is so much comfortable furniture available today that there's little excuse for buying a sofa that's too narrow for a nap or a chair with arms that keep your own akimbo. The secret to buying comfortable furniture is knowing a little about the subject, then trying the furniture before you buy it. A friend, who knows something about furniture, purchased a wicker chair that she had fallen in love with. With its tall, elegant back and high, curved arms, it was a work of art, a joy to behold. However, when she sat down in the chair to knit as she watched her favorite daytime TV program, she fell out of love. The arms were so high and so close, she couldn't maneuver her arms and wrists to knit. She still has the chair. How could she part with something so beautiful? But it no longer occupies the spot in which she likes to sit and knit. Task chairs should have low, open arms that allow freedom of movement.

Lounge chairs should allow you to lean back without strain. Your head should rest on the back of the chair. Your knees should not be restricted by the edge of the chair. The chair edge should be well padded and you should not be able to feel the wooden frame beneath. Your feet should touch the floor.

Recliners have been slicked up nine ways to Sunday, but most of them are still not cheerfully received in pretty living rooms. Call it snobbery, but they're still more at home in a den. Even comfortable, livable living rooms call for a nod to graciousness. Graceful rockers qualify. So do footstools of all sizes, ranging from giant, thirty-six-inch squares in all sorts of study fabrics and leathers to petite stools that tuck under a chair.

Assessing Quality

Quality upholstered pieces will have kiln-dried hardwood frames and hand-tied steel coil springs covered with layers of cotton batting and perhaps a quilted pillow of foam. This should be covered with muslin, then upholstery fabric. Patterns or grains of the finished upholstery fabric should be matched at seams and should align on pillows for an unbroken pattern. Pillow edges should align smoothly with one another, without gaps between them or the sofa seat or back. Pillows (especially a loose seat cushion) are generally attached to the sofa so as not to roll off. Look for wood finishes that are satin smooth to the touch and without discernible bubbles or blemishes to the eye. The sofa should not flex when it is picked up at either end, but should remain rigid and firm.

Selecting a Quality Sofa

Quality ensures a long-lasting sofa. The best sofas are custom-made by hand. Furniture makers construct a frame from zero-defect kiln-dried lumber (no knots to weaken support). Maple is the top pick because it does not become brittle with age. Less costly sofas will use other hardwoods or metal frames. Wood frames that are dowelled with corner blocks fastened with screws are most durable. Ask how coil springs are attached. Custom sofas feature coil springs that are hand tied. A webbing holds the bottom of the springs.

Filling, the stuff that makes a sofa comfy, can be polyester foam or fiberfill. Custom manufacturers use horsehair and burlap because it keeps its shape. Layers of cotton are stitched atop the filling, and in high-priced custom sofas, layers of goose down are added. Muslin covers the basic sofa structure and then upholstery is applied. The most durable fabrics are velvet, cotton, linen blends, and cotton chintzes. Leather lasts twice as long as fabric and also costs twice as much. Silk is an impractical choice as it is too fragile. Good sofas should last ten to fifteen years; great sofas last fifty or more.

Containing Living Room Noise

Any room designated for watching television should have a door. It's amazing how sound from TVs and radios carries throughout a house and especially up a stairwell. If you don't have a door, hang an old-fashioned portiere. These draperies will block the noise and can be pulled back out of the way when not in use. French doors block sound, but not the light or view, but they're expensive.

Hanging Artwork

The old eye-level rule works for hanging pictures because it places the subject where it can be seen with the least effort. A favorite technique is to hang pictures in groups or pairs for maximum impact. If you're cautious about exploring the possibilities, lay out your potential groups or pairs of pictures on the floor and experiment with different arrangements. Study the effect. Move one or more an inch this way, an inch that way, until your eye tells you that it's just right. Then, without having studded the wall with nail holes, you're ready to hang your composition.

Accessorizing for Comfort

Whether or not you add a lot of unnecessary but interesting items to your living room in order to cozy it up is probably a matter of personal style. Clutter is comforting to some, unnerving to others. Pillows, often used by magazine stylists to add color and pattern to what would otherwise be a relatively boring picture, are, more often than not, nusiances. They get pushed from one end of the couch to another by those seeking a comfortable spot. Some end up on the floor. Perhaps the thoughtful approach to the pillow problem involves placing a small wicker trunk or basket near the sofa. When you need a pillow for napping, you open the trunk and help yourself to a pillow. When you want it out of the way, you won't need to throw it on the floor. You can just pop it back in the basket.

Lamps

Believe it or not, some people hate lamps. They think lamps clutter up the scene and disrupt a sense of serenity. These people rely solely on track lights, wall sconces, and other built-in lighting. Others love lamps for both their functional and decorative value. There's nothing comfortable about a lamp that's too short to read by or so tall that the bulb shines in your eyes. A twenty-six-inch-high lamp is generally too short to use on an end table beside a sofa. In that case, a hefty stack of art books beneath the too-short lamp solves the problem handily. Just keep adding books and testing the results until you've added just the right number. If your lamp is too high, there's nothing to do but get a lower table or a different lamp. That's why adjustable lamps are such a godsend. They rise or lower to meet the occasion. They stoop to conquer, so to speak. Apothecary lamps—those small lamps on a slender metal pole—are flexible and attractive. They can be adjusted to any height and they fit very comfortably with both traditional and contemporary interiors.

Flooring

Some floorings are simply friendlier than others. Marble, new or antique, is off-putting. So is miles of white ceramic tile. Vinyl doesn't warm the heart. What does? Wood, the all-time, great, anywhere flooring is probably the most appealing and genuinely comfortable. Laid in planks and even some parquet patterns, it's enduringly warm. Area rugs add further warmth, color, and pattern. Oriental patterns do the best job of hiding wear and tear. Carpeting (not white) is also intimate and luxurious, and it's available in any price range. Wool gets a thumbs-up for high quality and durability. If wool carpeting is not within your budget, investigate installing synthetic carpeting, which is less expensive and easier to clean when it's been treated with protective coatings such as Scotchgard or Teflon.

Wall Coverings

The comfortable living room is serene. Often, to achieve it, we eschew pattern. We avoid the bold, brightly colored patterns so often found in wall coverings, but there are subtle patterns in complex neutral colors that add all the excitement necessary in a room intended for calm and order. There are also intriguing textures—linens, string weaves, burlaps, stone looks, metallics, and so forth—that add interest without introducing chaos or cuteness. Wall coverings enrich a plain surface in ways that no other material can. Hand-screened wall coverings (we don't call them wallpapers because they're not all paper, some are vinyl) are most expensive. Don't let that put you off, even if you're working on a tight budget. A small amount of an expensive wall covering can be used as an accent. A mural for one short wall needn't break the bank, either. Beautiful machine-made wall coverings are so plentiful that you should devote time to your search for the perfect pattern. Don't be dismayed by the sheer number of sample books you'll find at your local shop. Ask the salesperson for help in weeding out the unlikely books, then settle down for a long morning's hunt. Actually, you'll probably enjoy seeing the myriad patterns and colors available.

Simple snack or fancy feast, dining is the primary ritual of family and social life. Eating is more than the ingestion of food for survival. Instead, it is a rich experience of spiritual and physical nourishment. Eating is no longer confined to just the kitchen or dining room—it is an all-over-the-house affair. Meals are times for togetherness with family and friends where sharing feelings is as important as sharing sustenance. That no longer means strictly formal, sit-down functions.

Just as we have appetites for different types of food, we have appetites for different settings. To meet the needs of our moods, many homes have two just-for-eating places: one casual arrangement in the kitchen for quick, simple meals and one formal seating area set apart from the mechanics of food preparation for refined dining experiences.

The backbone of most entertaining is eating, even if it is not the primary reason why friends are over at your place. As good and thoughtful hosts, we must serve refreshments. As a result, eating happens just about anywhere in the house. During pleasant weather, our entertaining arena broadens to encompass the great outdoors. Patio, deck, by the pool, and under the trees become our spaces for informal meals.

Dining In

The essential equipment for dining is a table and chair, but dining really calls for just the right table and chair, not just any old table and chair, and all the other right stuff to meet the demands of the comfortable house. Keep in mind that all the background elements discussed earlier—good lighting, suitable color scheme, comfortable style—are part of the dining event.

All dining areas should have lights on a dimmer switch. Who wants to eat under lights as bright as those in an operating room? Dimmers are inexpensive, easily installed, and allow for greater flexibility. There are occasions when low light is preferred and times when bright light is a must. Some of your guests might need more light than others, so your dining room may need more than one source of light. Breakfast eating areas will need additional light for reading the newspaper and balancing early morning sunlight. For counters with high stools, place lights on

CHAPTER 9

Dining In/ Dining Out

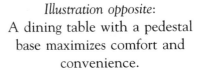

Illustration opposite:
A dining table with a pedestal base maximizes comfort and convenience.

tracks or recessed over each stool to both accent space and provide shadow-free illumination.

In the dining room, lighting functions not only to provide basic illumination, but also to establish mood and create a focal point. Chandeliers, the classic, elegant lighting icon, centered over the table, can provide a decorative element. Chandeliers, however, tend to direct light at the ceiling only, leaving a dark shadow under the center. To address this problem, some chandeliers have an additional down light positioned so that your centerpiece gets center stage. Additional lights should be used in areas where food is served and to fill in shadows around the perimeter of the room.

In some cases, you may simply want to forget all about the chandelier, since it roots the table to one spot and prohibits placement of the table anywhere else except beneath the chandelier. Consider other options such as wall sconces on each side of the room, recessed lighting, track lights, and lamps. These options provide attractive and diffuse light and do not interfere with arrangement of furniture. You may want to make the dining room table smaller than usual by removing its leaves so that you can place it next to the fireplace or piano for intimate and romantic dining. Chandelier or not, adequate and flexible illumination is a must for comfortable dining.

Functional furniture required for dining areas includes the essential table and chairs, console and storage cabinets for china and other equipment, and additional space for serving. There are a great variety of sizes and styles to meet your requirements. How much and what type of family dining and entertaining you do will certainly inform your choices.

When choosing a dining room table, you need some basic facts. How big is the room? How big is the actual usable space for table, chairs, and passage space? How many people need to be seated on a regular basis? How many people do you need to seat for a holiday or special event? There is an upper limit to how big a table can be for a particular room and a maximum number of people that can comfortably be seated. To find the maximum number of dinner guests, take the square footage of the dining room and divide by fourteen square feet. A typical ten- by twelve-foot room (120 square feet, divided by fourteen square feet) will accommodate eight guests. Space for a table, chairs, and serving aisles are included in this figure. Each chair requires two feet plus an additional two feet for manuevering around it. If the room has several doors and storage cabinets, fewer guests can be accommodated.

The best dining table for comfort and grace is round with a center pedestal to support the tabletop. Nothing is more miserable than sitting at a leg or being squeezed between a dinner companion and a table leg. Other uncomfortable table designs include tables with aprons (aprons restrict free movement of the legs), glass-topped tables (guests feel exposed if there is no tablecloth), and tables with more than four legs or legs that interfere with seating. When shopping for the most functional and comfortable dining table, take a seat at each place. Cross your legs at the knees and at the ankles. Move the chair in and out. Is every seating space as accommodating as the others?

The minimum edge space at a table that is needed for each diner is twenty-four to twenty-six inches per table setting, but thirty inches is ideal. The truly comfortable (and luxurious) amount of space per table setting is thirty inches. If space is at a premium, be sure to choose the round table with pedestal. Ovals and tables with corners or prominent table legs consume an additional eighteen inches of space. The standard heights for tables are thirty inches to thirty-two inches from the floor. Never try to fit a table that is too big into a space that is too small to accommodate too many people. Good food and good company can't compensate for discomfort.

For seating at dining tables, there are several options. Chairs should be functional; they must have the right seat height, the correct back design to support the body in an upright position, have the right arm height, and fit under the table. Just because a chair looks great pulled up to the showroom table does not mean it is comfortable. Test it for comfort. Sit in it. Scrunch and squirm. Is the seat wide enough to accommodate a larger-scaled person? The seat should have ample space on each side of the hip so that guests feel securely seated. The chair's seat should be deep but not so deep that the average diner's feet will dangle. (If your guest is smaller-scaled than average, provide a footstool.) The height of the seat should not be too high, nor should it be too low. Most occasional chairs intended for use in the living room are too low for a dining table. Many of us have experienced this in hotel dining rooms where, in the interest of the exotic, a well-meaning designer has selected low-slung chairs with high arms. Obviously, the designer never sat in that particular chair at that table. Chair backs should be high enough to support the upper back and shoulders. Most of us lean back slightly as we enjoy after-dessert coffee and conversation. Because we don't find it comfortable or practical to lean back while we are eating, a fairly straight-backed chair is best.

There should be adequate space between the chairs for easy maneuvering and psychological comfort. Some chairs, like side chairs and lounge chairs, are not designed for dining. When selecting chairs, consider how easy it will be for guests to slide the chair in and out from the table.

Some tables may call for a mix of armchairs and side chairs. You may opt for all armchairs or all side chairs, or decide on traditional armchairs for the hosts and side chairs for everyone else. The choice will be determined by your standards of comfort and the amount of space you have.

Chairs must be easy to maneuver over flooring. Several technologies exist that allow for adept manipulation of chairs. Look for gliders (they come designed for wood, tile, or carpet) and casters. If you already own your dining room chairs or have your heart set on a particular kind that has traditional legs, you can add gliders or casters. If you add casters, raise the table an equal number of inches to keep the chair and table proportions consistent. If not, the chair seat may suddenly be too high, resulting in squeezed thighs or constricted leg movement.

The most comfortable chairs are found in the office environment where furniture must perform, not just look pretty. As the office comes to look more like home, maybe the time has come for the home to borrow from the office. Big board room chairs work for dining rooms— they swivel, have casters for mobility, have high backs, and lumbar supports. They also adjust for tilt and pitch and arm and seat height for a totally custom and personal fit. The best chairs have an infinite range of adjustments, not just ratcheted points. Choose tufted, traditional Williamsburg or sleek contemporary styles in an array of handsome upholsteries and leathers. Not only do these chairs introduce a whole new level of comfort to your dining room, they probably do not cost more than the traditional, rigid, hard-to-move chair that ruins your carpet and causes awkward moments for your guests.

The way you entertain will also influence your furnishing choices. Is your entertaining sit-down or buffet or perhaps both? Consoles for storage and serving are usually required, particularly if you have more than one set of china and like to put out a number of serving dishes. Consoles should have a top with a minimum width of sixteen inches to hold chargers (they have a diameter of fourteen inches), dinner plates (they have a diameter of twelve inches), and serving platters. Measure your china and serving platters. What are the widest and tallest pieces your console must accommodate? Don't guess—simply take out the measuring tape and jot down the figures. Always shop with your tape measure to avoid disappointing surprises.

For informal eating, there is always the kitchen. Once again, a round table makes better use of space than a rectangular or square table since the absence of corners makes it easier to add an extra seat. Casual eating tables include a twenty-four-inch round bistro-style table for two and the more conventional forty-two to forty-eight-inch round table that seats four. If space allows, virtually any configuration can be used.

Kitchen designer Rudy Santos of Rosan Kitchens in New Providence, New Jersey, custom-made a round table with a pedestal base using the same Wilsonart solid-surface material for the table as for the kitchen countertops. The owners, inspired by the contemporary look, paired it with inexpensive office chairs on casters from IKEA—a perfect choice for rolling over the highly polished porcelain tile floor without a hitch or scratch.

Another team of interior designers remodeled a Hollywood home built in the '50s and chose to install a booth to create maximum eating space in the cramped kitchen. And yet another designer purchased an authentic butcher-block table at an antique shop that became both the breakfast table and cooking preparation center.

There are many quick and easy solutions to serving snacks and fast meals in or out of the kitchen. The pass-through, simply a portal cut out of a wall and equipped with a counter, or a peninsula, with its high counter, are practical methods of serving quick meals. Easy-maintenance, wipe-clean countertops make after-meal cleanup simple.

For seating, innovative designers are using drafting stools with adjustable heights at the counter. The high metal cage for footrests are a plus.

All of these examples illustrate the current trend toward a fusion of home and office. Designers and homeowners are considering all kinds of functional, comfortable alternatives. Stores such as IKEA, whose designers are really keen on flexibility, are leading the way toward new functionalism in furniture. We can enjoy the same kind of performance in our kitchen chair that we have grown accustomed to in our home office chair. It can even be the same chair.

We have learned from our jobs to do two or three tasks at once. Now we tend to do two or three things while we eat: watch TV or listen to the radio to get the news, make telephone calls (much to the chagrin of etiquette buffs), or scan the newspaper.

In a typical busy household where time and other resources are at a premium, think in terms of plain commonsense conveniences that will reduce setup and cleanup time. Dispense with tablecloths, placemats, and other time-consuming table settings, and opt for a tray that goes from kitchen to table and back again. Serving and cleanup time are minimized and children can handle it themselves.

A growing trend for families is to dine while watching television. Instead of gathering around the roaring fire of the hearth as families did in a previous century, today's family collects in front of what has symbolically become the new hearth, the television. Manufacturers, quick to pick up on the acceptability of this trend (it is now about forty years old) have created the high/low table that rises to the occasion. The table transforms from a low coffee table to a higher one at the turn of a lever. Also along these lines are benches on casters (our favorites are from IKEA) that do double duty as coffee tables or places to sit for informal snacking in the media room.

For breakfast, lunch, dinner, or a midnight snack in bed, there are new mobile side tables inspired by rolling hospital tables. The tabletop is supported by an arm that reaches across the bed from one side and is attached to a metal base with casters. Unlike traditional bed trays that rest on the bed, restrict leg movement, and are at risk of being upset, this type of bed tray allows for easy serving of food. The tray height is also adjustable. If you eat in bed regularly, use wall-hung lamps instead of bedside table lamps that will light up your eating area but leave plenty of space for storing the table.

Dining Out

Outdoor dining is the newest trend in eating. Restaurants, particularly in cities, are creating garden dining areas, sidewalk bistro tables, and patios to create a refreshing, new dining experience. Dining out of doors requires more than simply tossing a gingham cloth on the ground and settling down to a picnic of fried chicken and finger food. The new concept of outdoor dining takes a sophisticated approach and includes bringing outdoors all the comforts of home.

To dine outside successfully, some potentially discomforting obstacles must be overcome. These include the hot sun, bugs, wind, and sudden changes of weather as well as logistical problems of moving food from the kitchen to the great outdoors.

Shade from a merciless sun is the number-one problem. Umbrellas are not always large enough to solve the problem of providing adequate screening out of the sun's rays. Palm Beach resident Angie McNamara entertains out of doors year-round. She uses a sunshade for her patio meals. A bright blue plastic utility tarp with corner grommets (available at hardware stores) is suspended between the house on one end and tent poles at the other. The big four-foot by eight-foot instant awning covers the entire patio.

If you are willing to invest more in sun control, custom-made canvas sailcloth awnings can be made to order from a sail maker or awning supply company. The beauty of the custom-made awning is that you can select the colors and patterns and even design your own. Another way to reduce the sun's heat and glare involves building a pergola, a kind of extended, free-standing open-air porch, and planting it with trailing vines that will produce natural foliage shade within a few seasons.

For eating out of doors, you will need the essential dining furniture. Tables for outdoor use should have weep holes, slits, or openings in the table surface to allow rainwater to dissipate without damaging the table surface. A designer we know creates an instant and inexpensive portable table with a sheet of five-eighths-inch plywood supported by a pair of carpenter's sawhorses. For a festive and low-priced tablecloth, she covers her *al fresco* table with a king-sized sheet in a colorful pattern. To keep the cloth from flying away in the breeze, she ties the corners with bright ribbon bows. When the party is over, down comes the table for easy storage in the garage.

There are lots of chairs for outdoor dining, ranging from the very expensive wrought iron or aluminum and exotic (but more fragile) wicker to the very inexpensive plastic stackable chairs that cost six dollars and seem to be everywhere. The fact that they are cheap is not the only reason these chairs have taken the country by storm. They are comfortable! The shaped seat and back, unlike a perforated metal seat with woven nylon webbing, leave no unsightly marks. The chairs also come in a variety of colors.

If you entertain frequently on your deck or patio, perhaps you will need a California kitchen, a specially designed portable preparation and cooking station for outdoor use. The built-in, weatherproofed California kitchen features a work top, sink, a portable water source, under-counter minirefrigerator, a working grill, a wok, and additional burners for cooking. Some come replete with a dishwasher and storage space in the cabinet below the countertop for storing frequently used supplies such as candles (with globes to shield the flame from drafts), permanent centerpieces, and cooking and serving pieces. Designed to withstand the elements, the California kitchen can stay outdoors permanently.

If you plan on nighttime entertaining, plan for adequate electrical lighting, including overall illumination for the general area and, perhaps, special spotlights for the dining table. This can be augmented with candles and torches. You may also want to consider landscape lighting for safety and ambience. Illuminating walkways to and from the house is crucial for safety. The major concern at night is bug control. Short of screening in the porch or deck, other measures can reduce the presence of uninvited mosquitoes. Classic citronella candles keep bugs away and they cost very little. Electronic bug zappers are probably the most effective way to combat bugs. Another natural way to defeat bugs is to encourage bats to do the work. A single bat can ingest thousands of bugs nightly. Bat house kits are available through some garden supply stores.

One of the challenges of entertaining in the open air is getting the food, beverages, and all the supplies from the kitchen to their destination without incident. A sturdy metal tea cart will allow you to move from inside to outside efficiently. Outdoor furniture manufacturers also make carts that can stay outside permanently.

The key to outdoor dining is a take-it-easy approach. To set an attractive table, all that is required is the simplest and most natural centerpieces and decorations. Fresh flowers from your own yard, fresh fruit, and arrangements of garden-grown vegetables make totally satisfying centerpieces. We are most at home in the absence of artificiality and in the presence of these available and affordable elements of the natural world.

Dining In/Dining Out

Comfortable dining makes meals into enjoyable occasions for family and friends. The well-thought-out dining area—whether it is in the formal dining room, the kitchen, the patio, or even in front of the television—makes sharing meals meaningful. It turns the simple dinner into a stately pleasure.

CROWLEY '96

The kitchen is where we cook over open flames, manipulate sharp knives, handle heavy pots of scalding water, strain to reach high shelves, and stand on our heads to retrieve skillets hidden in the recesses of low, dark places. Sometimes we walk endless miles to prepare just one meal. There's no doubt about it, a poorly designed kitchen can be more than uncomfortable, it can be downright dangerous. It is worth the time and effort to plan a kitchen that is safe and convenient—a truly comfortable place.

CHAPTER 10

The Kitchen

New Design Rules

The National Kitchen and Bath Association (NKBA), an organization that certifies kitchen designers as professionals (CKDs), published a new kitchen design guide in 1992. Times had changed. The last clear guidelines were formulated in 1945 and worked just fine for stay-at-home moms who cooked alone in a kitchen where about 400 items were stored.

The kitchen design experts who worked on the new guide recognized a number of significant social and other changes that directly affect kitchen planning. For starters, few of us cook alone in our kitchens. There are multiple users of the kitchen who range in age and ability, and often families enjoy cooking (as well as eating) together. We store about 800 items—twice as many food products as our grandmothers. We also cook differently than our grandmothers did fifty years ago. We use more fresh, refrigerated, and frozen foods, and as a result, we need more refrigerator and freezer space.

New appliances, including microwave ovens, convection ovens, woks, grills and griddles, and so forth have changed our cooking habits. We may cook and freeze meals on weekends, then defrost and cook them in a microwave on weekdays. For that reason, having a microwave oven near the table is convenient and creates a natural second work center for a second cook or cook's helper.

Today's kitchen architecture is as innovative as the latest cooking technology and fits our new, flexible lifestyles. It adds to our sense of comfort in the kitchen. Fifty years ago, kitchens were dark caves lit by a single circular fluorescent tube. Now, thanks to new trends in glass and window design, our kitchens can feature whole walls of windows. Skylights and open floor plans create spaces that are a joy to use.

In the past, kitchens in big houses were the provinces of hired cooks, and kitchens in smaller homes were not considered important rooms but purely utilitarian places. Today, most of us spend a great deal of time in our kitchens, which are likely to be as big as we can possibly afford. We have more room for architectural elements such as islands, window seats, built-in desks, bookcases, and fireplaces. We do all we can to make our kitchens not only great work spaces but natural gathering spots for family and friends. Whether you're building a new house or remodeling an older one, using the services of a professional or doing it yourself, familiarizing yourself with these National Kitchen and Bath Association's new design guidelines will help ensure that your kitchen will have every safety and convenience feature:

• Getting Around

The kitchen is the busiest room in the house. The cook is seldom, if ever, alone. Usually there are plenty of people around assisting, cleaning up, or popping in and out. To handle the traffic without jams or collisions, forget about the old thirty-inch-wide doorway. Entries should be at least thirty-two inches wide, and more spacious thirty-four-inch to thirty-six-inch doorways are even better. Traffic paths through kitchens should be at least thirty-six inches wide. If two are cooking or the main thoroughfare is also a work aisle, make the aisle forty-eight inches to sixty inches wide.

• The Geometry of Comfort

A kitchen setup is organized as a work triangle. This triangle is formed by dividing the kitchen equipment into three groups by function: storage and preparation, waste management, and cooking. The refrigerator, food storage, and preparation space forms one leg; the sink, dishwasher, garbage, and recycling area the second; and the oven, stove, and microwave the third. If you were to analyze your own kitchen by drawing an imaginary line connecting the three points, you will see the triangle.

The work triangle is a shorthand way to describe how each piece of kitchen equipment relates to the other. There are many different standard configurations, and each type has particular advantages for different individuals. Some work triangles are easier to navigate than others, particularly for physically challenged people. Your kitchen's work triangle may be almost a straight line or it may be a squat or elongated triangle, but the idea is still the same. The key features must be arranged so that getting food from one spot to the next is effortless.

The most efficient configuration, consisting of the refrigerator, sink, and oven, is generally laid out in a triangle that totals less than twenty-six feet, with no one leg of the triangle shorter than four feet or longer than nine feet. The idea is to place these major appliances in close enough proximity so that cooking and serving is easier, but not so close that performing simultaneous tasks is impossible.

One prime example of a how *not* to lay out a kitchen comes from a $3 million home in Palm Beach, Florida. The capacious kitchen seemed to have everything—it had been especially designed for multiple professional cooks and for entertaining scores of people—but the designer had failed to heed one very basic rule. The dishwasher and oven had been installed directly across from one another along a narrow aisle so that when the door of one was down, there was no room for the other to open. Nor could anyone even move past whoever was standing in proximity to either appliance. Not even one cook could work effectively, much less two or the whole family. Appliances should be staggered so that this never happens. Aisles should be wide enough to accommodate two people. To avoid collisions with the cook, the work triangle should not be a thruway. Traffic should be routed around this crucial work space.

The work triangle is a basic concept that has been used in kitchen design for decades. The standard kitchen formats are referred to as the U-shape, L-shape, island, peninsula, corridor, and pullman. All these arrangements depend upon how much kitchen space is available. The more space, the more options you have with work triangles.

The U-shape is commonly encountered in small, square kitchens. The sink is flanked on one side by a refrigerator and the other by the stove to form a U. Each side is at a right angle. Long, rectangular kitchens are generally L-shaped, with the sink and cooking equipment on the

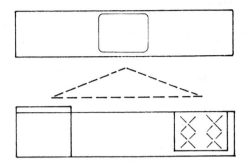

Pullman

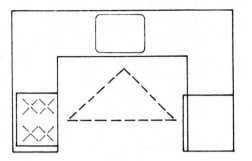

U-shape

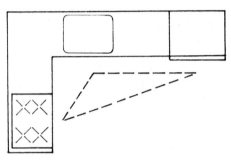

L-shape

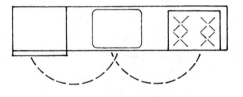

Corridor

These basic kitchen
plans illustrate the flow
of movement within the
work triangle —from
refrigerator to sink to
stove.

long wall and the refrigerator on the short wall. The U- and L-shaped formats are common in kitchens in which space is at a premium.

The corridor and Pullman designs are more linear. If the kitchen space is long, almost like a hallway, then these two layouts are the only options. The corridor places equipment and appliances along each side of the room. A typical kitchen in the corridor plan would have a refrigerator, sink, and work space along one side, and the stove, oven, and additional work space along the opposite wall. The Pullman, named for the efficient kitchens found on trains, places the sink, refrigerator, and stove all along the same wall.

Island and peninsula kitchens feature free-standing cabinets and equipment in the center of the kitchen (the island), or a long extension of cabinets and countertops that extends into the room. Islands and peninsulas call for either larger kitchens or a willingness to sacrifice open but underutilized space.

For those larger, more heavily equipped kitchens, the new *soft geometry* sets up two or three work triangles. In these cases, to avoid collisions, legs of two triangles may coincide, but must not overlap, according to the new design guide. The soft geometry approach enables a number of people to work in a kitchen without bumping into each other. This is especially helpful if the family cooks together or entertains on a grand scale.

It is possible to set up two work triangles even in a long, narrow kitchen. A Pullman style kitchen in a renovated Federal-style home in Summit, New Jersey, featured a refrigerator, a length of counter space for the main sink/disposal/dishwasher, additional space for cooking, and a stove. At the far end of the counter was a small bar sink that came in handy for morning coffee making and nightly cleanup. The one flaw was that the bar sink was at the opposite end from the refrigerator, causing coffee lovers to troop back and forth from one end to the other for cream. To better utilize the setup, the ideal solution would be to install a small refrigerator/ice-maker under the bar sink, a real plus for entertaining.

• A Place for Everything

Hunting for a special tool wastes time and can make the cook boil over. How much storage space is required? The rule of thumb is to provide at least 144 inches of wall cabinet frontage (or equivalent) in kitchens of 150 square feet. If your kitchen is bigger, provide 192 inches of wall cabinet frontage. For true convenience, cabinets should be within a short reach of the sink or at least close enough for easy storage and retrieval of dishes. The new guidelines recommend sixty inches of wall cabinet frontage within seventy-two inches of the primary sink center-line. To make sure you'll have enough cabinet and countertop space, simply measure along the front of the cabinets or do some simple math and multiply the counter width by the number of cabinets.

Cabinets come in a variety of dimensions and feature customizable options. Take advantage of special drawers with interior vertical dividers and shelves with pull-out drawers, drawer/roll-out space, or swing-out pantries. These are all designed with comfort in mind. Specialized cabinetry reduces excessive bending or having to get on hands and knees to find a pot or pan.

• Work Tops

Adequate work surfaces are a must. Give yourself plenty of counter space flanking the sink, refrigerator, cook top (or range), and oven. You need at least fifteen inches on one side of a refrigerator (preferably both), eighteen inches beside a cook top, and twenty-four inches beside the sink. You may get by with a little less on the opposite sides of all three of these work centers, but be as generous as space allows.

Countertops can be of any material, from wood to tile to laminated material, but some materials offer better comforts and conveniences than others. Ceramic tile, although quaint and charming, is not a comfortable surface if you chop and dice frequently. If you already have tile, simply place a folded cloth under your cutting board to make cutting easier. Marble is beautiful and very costly but, according to gourmet cooks, it can be difficult to maintain. It is so porous that water and fruit juices make permanent stains. Wood and laminates are excellent materials for countertops. Some cooks like laboratory countertops made of slate. Laminates are used widely, are reasonably priced, and come in a wide variety of beautiful colors and patterns.

• Quick, Easy Cleanup

Locate your dishwasher within thirty-six inches of the sink, and where it is accessible to a helper. Whether the dishwasher is to the right or left of the sink is not important. For ready access to the dishwasher, leave about two feet of space (or more) between it and another appliance so that one person working at the dishwasher does not get in the way of another. Don't locate the dishwasher near the counterspace designated for food preparation (that is the thirty-six inches of countertop to one side of the sink). A dishwasher placed smack-dab in the middle of the food prep area makes it impossible to load and unload the dishwasher without disrupting any work in progress.

Waste disposal strategies also influence kitchen design. Recycling is the law in most communities, so instead of needing one garbage can under the sink, we now need three containers to handle all the rubbish. Even in major cities, garbage disposals are back in favor. Plan for a waste receptacle for general garbage and containers for glass, aluminum cans, steel cans, cardboard, newspapers, and plastics. Placing these bins in the kitchen makes the most sense, but if your kitchen is small, you may have to set up a system in the garage, basement, or any other spot near the kitchen.

• General Health, Safety, and Comfort Features

For good ventilation and natural light, window and skylight square footage should equal or exceed 10 percent of the area of the kitchen. One of the biggest changes over the decades has been in the increased demand for natural light. No longer content with the one window over the sink, homeowners are opting for window walls to let all the sun in that they can. Most homeowners will tell you that they feel much happier when sunlight floods into the kitchen in the morning, particularly in winter when the days are short. If you are planning for lots of windows, make sure that there is ample and flexible artificial lighting installed to prevent unacceptable areas of shadow and glare. For more information on planning your lighting scheme, see chapter five.

Open windows help to remove smoke and odors, but no matter how many windows you have, you will still need the best quality ventilation system you can get. Equip cooking surface appliances with an exterior-exhaust ventilation system with a fan rated at 150 cubic feet per minute (CFM) or higher. Do not place a cook top or range below an operable window if you intend to use the window frequently, and allot a margin of three inches behind the appliance and a clearance over the stove of twenty-four inches to prevent burns.

Ask your electrician to have more than one circuit for the kitchen, especially if you entertain a lot and will be running the microwave, electric skillets, coffee urns, and other equipment all at the same time. You'll need ground fault circuit interrupters (they automatically interrupt the flow of electricity if an appliance is dropped in water) for electrical appliances located within six feet of a water source. Also, plan for a number of easy-to-reach electrical outlets. Install a fire extinguisher near the stove and a smoke alarm just outside the kitchen. For more information about kitchen design guidelines and to find the name of the Certified Kitchen Designer nearest you, write the National Kitchen and Bath Association, Dept. HM1092, 68 Willow Grove St., Hackettstown, NJ 07840.

Easygoing Appliances and Fixtures

Not so long ago, professional-caliber stoves, convection ovens, and extra-quiet and fancy-featured faucets were exclusively high-priced, European-made models. In the quest for speed, energy conservation, and ease of operation, mainstream consumers have created a demand for higher performance appliances. New, more moderately priced appliances offer many of the same performance features as European models.

Professional ranges for home use are still rare. They are not only costly, but require special insulation. These ranges are so heavy that the floor has to be boosted to prevent sagging joists. There are a whole new array of professional-style stoves made especially for residential use. They come in popular thirty-inch widths as well as thirty-six-inch and forty-eight-inch sizes. Prices start around $2,000 and go as high as $8,000, but nothing beats them for cooking performance.

Technologically advanced residential ranges offer a staggering array of conveniences as well as cooking and cleanup features (such as self-cleaning abilities, sealed gas burners, or smooth tops that hide electric coils) and cost about $150 to $200 more than standard conventional models. Despite their slightly higher cost, smooth tops are so easy to care for that they're fast becoming the range top of choice, replacing sealed-burner models. Unlike induction models (coils that produce high-frequency alternating magnetic fields in cookware, so that only the pan is heated), smooth tops require no special, high-priced cookware. Smooth tops so are named because the stove surface is one seamless piece. Flexibility is a priority in cook top design.

Ovens are getting bigger and more efficient. Convection ovens (with radiant heat elements and a circulating fan at the rear of the oven that moves air around for even cooking) cook meats up to 30 percent faster than conventional ovens. This time-saving type of oven is no longer available only at the high end. Magic Chef's TimeSavor range/oven combines conventional radiant heat with low-level microwave power and cuts cooking time in half.

Microwave ovens come in so many different styles and combinations that it's impossible to discuss them all in detail. Just know that whatever you dream up for your personal convenience is probably available and worth shopping for. Some cooks have already discovered the advantages of having two microwaves, one in each food preparation area. Micro-waves mounted in base cabinets are easier for children and those in wheelchairs to operate.

Refrigerators offer more and more comfort features, including shelves inside the doors for gallon-sized milk and beverage containers and see-through shelves and doors for quick-pick sodas. In-door ice and water dispensers are time and energy savers. New models are better insulated and designed for energy efficiency. Models that are only twenty-four inches deep fit flush with cabinet fronts for a sleeker look. Some even allow you to put in cabinetry fronts. The new design elements mean kitchens no longer have to look like laboratories. Kitchen appliances now can be customized with rounded edges for a furniture-like look that's more suitable for open kitchens.

Dishwashers are quieter than ever, prompted by the popularity of open kitchens and great rooms. Additionally, you can add insulation inside the cabinet cavity and mount the dishwasher on an insulation board. For more sound reduction tips, see chapter four.

Electronic controls that are complicated to use are neither convenient nor comfortable. Look for appliances with user-friendly, preprogrammed, one-button controls. For example, the latest technology in electronic pilotless gas stoves eliminates the pilot light that burns twenty-four hours a day.

Water purifiers have become increasingly popular. Available in different configurations, most use single-stage or two-stage filtration. The single-stage filter uses activated charcoal. The two-stage filter uses activated charcoal plus a second filter to eliminate harmful trace chemicals. If you have an automatic ice maker, make sure that the water is filtered first for better ice cubes.

Don't overlook instant hot water dispensers. They're environmentally sound because they keep a small amount of water heated at about 190 degrees Fahrenheit, saving energy needed to boil water as needed.

Convenient, Space-Saving Appliances

Convenience is the key feature in new, space-saving, small appliances. Horizontal toasters are extra wide and deep for toasting bagels. Standup mixers lock in place in upright and mixing positions. Double-batch mixers mix two boxes of chocolate chip cookies at once. Blenders have 21,000 rpm action and special blades. Microwave oven directions are available by pressing a key for programming hints. They're all designed to make your time in the kitchen—one of the two most vital rooms in any home—altogether pleasant.

Easy-Keep, Easy-Use Cabinets

You may have the most up-to-date appliances, but if your kitchen cabinets aren't equally painless, your kitchen's not going to be your favorite room. For long-time satisfaction, buy the best you can afford. Essentially, there are two kinds of cabinets: framed and frameless. The framed type shows the frame beyond the cabinet door. The door completely covers the frameless type. Generally, cabinets with frames look more traditional and rustic. Frameless cabinets look more contemporary.

Other than that, both types come in various materials and finishes. Mid-price cabinets use particleboard while higher-priced cabinets use plywood substrates laminated with vinyl foil, Melamite, or high-pressure plastic. High-priced cabinets are usually wood. Check drawer construction to determine how well the cabinets are made. The drawer is a four-sided box with a finished face, an open top, and a bottom that fits into dadoes in the drawer sides. A well-made drawer has solid hardwood sides and a plywood bottom. The wood should be well sanded and smooth to the touch. Slides should be heavy-duty, silent, with little or no side-to-side movement. For greatest convenience, get slides with full-drawer extension. Similarly, choose steel hinges that permit you to open cabinet doors as wide as possible. Finally, finishes are important. Check to see that there are no bubbles in laminated finishes (they may already be delaminating) or ripples in painted finishes. Wear only adds to the appeal of antique painted finishes, but, if the latest in high-tech finishes is your cup of tea, consider a catalyzed varnish similar to urethane coating. Synthetic resins are heat-cured for a finish that even nail polish remover won't affect.

Provide a Place for Snacking

For a truly comfortable kitchen, provide a place to sit down for a cup of morning coffee or a late-night snack. Islands, counters, and peninsulas are all great solutions when space is limited. Usually, they're thirty-six inches high—the same as a kitchen counter. If you dislike the high stools necessary for these counters, you can build in one at table height and use a chair. The minimum width for a countertop is fifteen to eighteen inches. Countertops that are extensions of the kitchen counter will be twenty-four inches wide. A tablelike peninsula can be café table width (thirty inches), a standard forty-two inches, or bigger, if you like. Surfaces can match the kitchen countertop, if they're the same height. If your snack counter is lower than the kitchen counter, use a different surface material.

The Look of Comfort

One important component of blissful comfort is making room for things that mean a lot to you. For one woman designing her dream kitchen, storing a basket collection was one problem that turned into an opportunity. Her baskets, which she used for picking fresh vegetables from the garden and for serving hot breads for meals, were hung on S-hooks from an antique ship's chain suspended from a corner ceiling hook. The arrangement added a warm touch and was compatible with her rustic barn board cabinets.

There is something very satisfying about coming home to a place that's in some way uniquely your own. No matter whether you choose a country, traditional, modern, art deco, French Provincial, eclectic, clutter, or uncluttered style, the guidelines offered here will provide the basic creature comforts that make your kitchen the warm and welcoming heart of your home.

Another key to personal comfort is to select the style that's right for your circumstances. In a Summit, New Jersey, kitchen, this meant designing a new, one-wall kitchen. Ordinarily, one-wall configurations are not encouraged because they're not as convenient as the L-or U-shape or even a pullman plan. In this case, the arrangement was necessary in order to leave room for a breakfast area.

Because the house was an eighteenth-century Federal style, frameless cabinets with classic raised ground panels were installed. The surface was classic white wipe-clean foil. The solid-surface countertop looked like granite but was much less expensive. Knobs were easy-to-grasp egg-shaped solid brass. French doors that led to the front hall and dining room were compatible with the style of the house. Big, double-hung windows with easy-to-clean, removable grilles added light and gave the kitchen a garden-room feeling.

Although all cabinets and appliances were placed along one long wall, two sinks (one at either end) were included.

Two years after the remodeling, the owners were unexpectedly transferred out of state. A potential buyer, an architect, told them, "I not only *love* your kitchen, I envy you it." Even though the owners had decided to redo the kitchen during a downturn in local real estate prices, it paid off handsomely. Not only was it wonderfully livable, it prompted a bidding war between two determined buyers who recognized and responded to its thoughtful comforts.

Light can make all the difference between a comfortable and uncomfortable kitchen. A friend, Norma Andrews, was not happy with her kitchen. After making a list of the things she liked and disliked about it, she discovered that she liked the knotty pine cabinets, the blue-and-white wallpaper, the patterned floor, and even the location of her appliances. What she did not like was the kitchen's small windows. They made her kitchen so dark and gloomy that she was reluctant to spend time there, even though she loved to cook. She switched the three double-hung windows for a floor-to-ceiling bay window that added light and space. The change from a dark to a light and inviting kitchen seemed almost miraculous. Now, this kitchen—chock-full of antique shop finds and the owner's colorful needlework—is where the whole family gravitates.

Comfort is so vital that some of us don't hesitate to go to what others would consider an extreme. For one young couple we know, this meant excavating to lower the floor (hence, raise the ceiling) in the ground-floor kitchen of a New York City brownstone. To another editor friend, adding a short peninsula counter in one corner of her kitchen will give her a landing place for pots and pans from her kitchen stove and a place to perch for a quick cup of tea. The cost? Perhaps a hundred dollars and a trip to Home Depot for a tall base cabinet to serve as the peninsula base and to arrange to have a countertop built to fit. The payoff? It's hard to put a price tag on that kind of comfort.

House Comfortable Tip: How to Customize a Tall Kitchen Cabinet

Most standard tall cabinets are laid out in space-wasting ways. A standard tall cabinet outfitted top to bottom with solid shelves has almost the same storage volume as a standard base cabinet of the same width but half the height, according to the National Kitchen and Bath Association. Standard setups work only if 90 percent of your meals come from cans!

Deep, dark shelves hide lots of things. Another space waster: the standard broom closet with one top shelf and one huge cavity that scrambles stuff together.

Tailor your tall cabinet to meet your specific storage and convenience needs. Customizing a tall cabinet enlarges storage capacity by as much as three times. Planning is the key to truly customized storage.

The procedure is simple: Measure every item you plan to store. Then, using these dimensions, sketch your storage plan on graph paper. You'll be able to see where and how everything will fit and plan for the exact amount of shelving, baskets, and racks that you'll need. For the most satisfactory results, don't try to shortcut the process. It gives you time to think before you buy.

Take your information with you when you shop. Storage space organizing systems are available from a number of manufacturers and retailers, including specialty stores that stock only shelving and storage supplies. Manufactured storage systems offer organizing aids, including shelving, rods, racks, bins, baskets, and accessories that make customization easy and relatively inexpensive. You can buy open stock components from your local home center, department store, or specialty store, and install them yourself.

Ventilated wire systems (with either an epoxy or vinyl coating over a steel rod) are popular and effective. Open stock wire components include shelves and hanging rods in eighteen-inch, thirty-inch, and forty-two-inch lengths, and stacking baskets in single, double, and triple-drawer depths. Accessory items include small door/wall racks in assorted sizes, including one deep enough to hold folded paper grocery bags. Choose from open (one-inch square) or tight (one-half inch by one inch) mesh construction that prevents small items from slipping through the cracks. A typical eighteen-inch-wide pantry can be fitted with four linen shelves, a deluxe basket system (a three-basket stacked unit), and a floor-to-ceiling door/wall rack for approximately $110.

The Cutting Edge of Universal Design

In 1992, Diane Pilgrim, director of the Cooper-Hewitt National Museum of Design, wrote: "Forty-three million Americans are disabled. Our world has been designed for young, certain height and weight, right-handed, hearing, seeing. . . . For the aging and the ill, the world is an obstacle course. Much of the designed world disables people by exclusion." Ms. Pilgrim, a sufferer of multiple sclerosis, knew firsthand the challenges faced by people in walkers and wheelchairs.

Universal design means making space accessible to the widest possible universe of users. Universal design is good design: it is humane, democratic, functional, affordable, and esthetically enhancing. Design excellence is a cultural, social, and economic imperative.

Universal design accommodates a range of disabilities. What factors, physical and cognitive, might restrict performance? Wheelchair, crutches, canes, and walkers call for wide aisles, lower counters, under-counter knee space, and easy reaching distances. Can the user fully extend, bend, and lift arms, legs, or hands? Limited reach and grip also influence design.

The principles of universal design take into account the varying height of the general population. Designers assume that the average person is in the range of five feet one inch to six feet zero inches. Universal design acknowledges that high or low reach adjustments might be necessary.

Limited hearing and vision also may call for modifications of machinery and appliances. Limited feeling in hands or legs can prevent a person from knowing if they are burned, bruised, or cut. Allowances must be made for distance and positioning of appliances and obstacles.

Are the user's cognitive faculties limited? Limited memory or other mental impairments might make completing a task difficult. Equipment within the home must be easy to operate and the environment (bedroom, bathroom, kitchen, or laundry facilities) must be as orderly as possible. This is the goal of the universal designer.

To make a kitchen comfortable for everyone—young, old, and in-between, able-bodied or infirm—many are looking to universal design criteria. The concept is simple: create spaces that meet the needs of the least able user, who may have impaired vision, hearing, manual dexterity, or mobility. Of course, if the disabled can use these spaces easily and with fewer accidents, so can everyone else. Universal kitchen design ideas and criteria include the following:

- Pull-out spray faucets with button controls on the handle are easy to operate in both the kitchen and bath. These should retract easily when not in use.
- Doorways should be thirty-four to thirty-six inches wide and provide a clear width of thirty-two inches for wheelchair passage. Doorways should have no saddles so that chairs can roll through

easily. It is difficult for a person in a wheelchair to back up, and both wheelchairs and walkers require a turning radius of sixty inches. Make allowance for this, especially at an entry, where the person in a chair or walker must enter, then turn around to close the door. Keep this turn-around area clear. For wheelchairs and walkers, whenever possible, eliminate doors. They're troublesome to open, pass through, and then close. When doors must be used, consider pocket doors. If doors must be hinged, fit them with lever handles.

- If possible, make aisles in kitchens a minimum of four feet wide. Then, a walker or wheelchair can easily negotiate the space without difficult maneuvering and turning. In an older kitchen, you may not be able to change aisle widths, but keep new cabinet runs and islands short so that a walker or wheelchair can maneuver without having to turn around.

- When it comes to flooring, select a nonskid surface. Resilient floorings should not be so light as to show scuff marks, nor so dark as to reduce visibility. If you're using carpeting, use no padding at all or a thin padding that will not hinder a chair or walker.

• Easy on the Eyes

A kitchen designed especially to accommodate a disabled member of the family need not look much different than any other—at least, at first glance. For example, considerations made for wheelchair-bound users, such as lowered work counters, will not be visibly obvious and will benefit those who wish to sit while they perform kitchen tasks. The tips that follow will also benefit others in the family.

• Easy-Access Refrigerators and Freezers

Store foods in a side-by-side refrigerator and freezer, which is easier to roll a wheelchair near. Narrow doors are easier for young people and the elderly to handle. See-through shelves and drawers make it quicker and easier for everyone to identify contents. These should roll out for easy access. A model with a through-the-door ice maker and water dispenser eliminates the need to open the door.

• Comfortable Food Preparation Centers and Cabinets

Include a twenty-nine-to thirty-inch-high counter with knee space underneath. Omit under-sink cabinetry so that a wheelchair can roll into this space, since sitting and working sideways is awkward and inconvenient. Fit this food preparation and cleanup area with its own shallow sink that is five and one-half to six inches deep and about thirty inches high. Add a hot water dispenser for instant soups and other quick-meal preparations. (This eliminates the use of hot pots, which are dangerous for children, the elderly, and the infirm.)

Other base cabinets should have ten-inch-deep by eight- to ten-inch-high recesses for toe kick areas, to allow for wheelchair footrests. Omit cabinet doors whenever possible for convenient access. Fit necessary storage cabinet doors with easy-open magnetic latches. Install lazy susans and pull-out drawers, shelves, and bins wherever possible.

• Convenient Cook Centers

Fit thirty-inch-high cook center countertops with cook tops or ranges with front-mounted, easy-to-reach knobs, handles, or controls large enough to be easily manipulated. Some experts advise against using gas appliances with open flames. An adjustable mirror above the cook top will enable children or a wheelchair-bound cook to see into deep pots. Those in wheelchairs need handy landing spots for pots and pans at drawer height, so consider installing pull-out shelves. Place one on each of the base cabinets flanking a thirty-inch-high cook top. Install switches for vent hoods at countertop height and near the front of the counter so that they'll be low enough to be easily accessed by those in wheelchairs.

Install microwave and other ovens at the thirty-inch height. Pick models with controls that are easily reached and manipulated and doors that open wide for easy loading and removing of pots. Leave a minimum of fifteen inches of countertop landing space for hot dishes.

• Cleanup Centers

Cleanup areas should have shallow sinks (like those in food preparation centers). They're more easily reached by any seated worker who may not be wheelchair-bound but simply lacks the strength to stand for long periods of time. Raise the dishwasher six to eighteen inches above the floor for easier access by those in a chair, and leave eighteen to twenty-four inches on each side so it can be reached from either side. Anyone who needs to sit while doing food preparation or cleanup chores benefits from an open-based countertop and a fully outfitted sink.

Universal Design Facts

- A wheelchair requires four and a half to five and a half feet for turning.
- Doorway clearing for wheelchairs and walkers must be thirty-two inches. Add two inches more for the door itself. The opening should be thirty-four inches wide.
- Walkers need a turning radius of four to five feet.
- Comfortable reach down and forward for people in a wheelchair is twenty to twenty-four inches.
- Work areas will be major food preparation areas with ample countertop, a large sink, cook top, and so forth.
- Satellite work areas may be specialty work centers; that is, a salad making center, bake center, and so forth.

The Work Triangle

Some configurations favor certain conditions and not others. Modifications can be made to accommodate need. The distance between the sink and appliances is crucial for those moving on crutches or walkers. Great distances will tire them. Shortening the distances helps eliminate inefficiencies for everyone.

A U-shaped work center is best for . . .

- Wheelchair
- Two people
- Traffic flow reduction
- Reducing risk of bumping into appliances

A U-shaped work center does not work well for people with maneuvering difficulty, difficulty seeing across wide-open spaces, walkers, crutches, or low vision.

An L-shaped work center is best for . . .

- Traffic flow
- Storage next to workstations
- Two people or a wheelchair

An L-shaped work center does not work well for people with maneuvering difficulty, difficulty seeing across wide open spaces, walkers, crutches, or low vision.

To adapt your kitchen, place the cooking workstation closer to the corner of the L.

An island or peninsula work center is best for . . .

- People with walkers, crutches, or low vision because it shortens the work triangle for easy use

It does not work well for those in wheelchairs, as appliances block the aisle.

To adapt your kitchen for a wheelchair, move the island/peninsula farther away from the main wall to increase aisle space.

A corridor or Pullman work center is best for . . .

- Walkers, crutches, and low vision, because it shortens the work triangle for easy use
- Corridor: appliances are across the aisle from each other
- Pullman: appliances are along the same wall

It does not work well for people in wheelchairs, as open appliance doors block the aisle.

To adapt your kitchen, widen aisle space.

Selecting the Right Materials

Understand product benefits and how to use readily available materials. Floor covering improves mobility and aids vision. Use bold patterns and borders at boundaries to set off key work spaces. Border contrast is especially helpful for low vision and, for people with limited memory, it is a spatial organizer.

Floors for Better Mobility
- Choose stain-resistant carpet with a smooth surface for easier cleaning.
- Use contrasting borders on the floor to warn low-vision users of changes.
- Carpeted flooring and padding muffle noise and improve hearing appliance signals.
- Noncarpeted flooring lets users hear people entering or leaving the room.
- No-wax vinyl or ceramic floorings are too dangerous for crutches and walkers.
- High-pile carpet prohibits wheelchair movements.
- Hardwood is slippery and provides no traction for dogs.
- Use plain or muted patterned floors so that dangerous spills may be spotted easily.
- Very light-colored flooring shows scuff marks from wheels or canes.
- Use light to midvalue range colors because dark colors reduce visibility in a room.

Wall Coverings
- Wall coverings function as room maps for those with low vision. Use color-coded wallpapers or painted treatments.
- Use wall coverings that hide fingerprints for householders with

vision impairment and for those who use the walls to balance themselves.

- Large wallpaper patterns and bright colors are most effective for those with vision and depth perception problems.
- Distinguish doors, cabinets, and hallways with color.
- Use wallpaper with appropriate motifs (like food designs in the kitchen) for each room for those who are memory impaired or have cognitive difficulties.
- Contrast paint trim for receptacles, light switches, and doors.
- Use a change in pattern or color to orient people toward activities. Use blue paint or paper over the cold water faucet and red over the hot faucet.

Countertops

Countertop design and materials can reduce or prevent problems.

- Adjust the height of workstations so you can sit down on the job.
- Round edges of countertops reduce chance of injury.
- Contrast countertop edges to indicate where they end.
- Install a grab bar for balance at edge of the countertop.

More on Comfortable Cabinetry

- Match cabinet features to special needs. This costs more, but it saves time and effort.
- Use egg-shaped handles for easy grip.
- Use self-closing doors to prevent mishaps.
- Put objects in easy reach with pull-out shelving.
- Extra-sturdy, covered drawers can be used for stepping stools under the sink, wall ovens, or the cook top.
- Use color-coded cabinet pulls.

Lighting Specifics for the Kitchen

- Think in terms of high levels of illumination for safety.
- Light cabinets and insides of closets.

- Natural light is more diffuse and provides better light than artificial.
- Optimize the use of natural lights from skylights, windows, and other natural light sources.
- Install timers or motion detectors to automatically turn on the lights.
- Install warning lights for the hearing impaired.
- Adjustable overhead lamps work best for families with height variations.
- Reduce glare by using fluorescent lights and soft-light incandescents.
- Call the American Lighting Association at 800/274-4484 for more information.

Turn to chapter seventeen for more information on Universal Design and a list of pertinent organizations and resources.

The bedroom is a sanctuary. The most private and personal quarters of your home, it is the room where you spend most of your time—one-third of your life to be exact—and should be planned for total rest and relaxation of body and soul. We need to feel soothed, calmed, and restored within the boundaries of this intimate world where the daily rituals of our private life take place.

The design should reflect your most personal needs for comfort and function. Bedrooms must do more than simply house the bed in which we sleep. The factors that define the room's function include age, interests, sleeping patterns, number of persons sharing the room, and their relationship. The bedroom also must have some type of seating for simple relaxation, reading, and perhaps conversation. A must for today's bedrooms is a television as most of us enjoy watching television to wake us up and get us up to speed with the rest of the world or to provide some background sound for dozing off to sleep. Another amenity that is quickly becoming a necessity is a stereo (or at least a radio).

Most rooms will need to facilitate basic sleeping and grooming functions, but beyond that, couples, siblings, and singles each have different requirements for comfort. These extra functions of the bedroom determine the furnishings needed and even the bedroom's style. When planning bedrooms, consider all the factors of comfort as well as sleep patterns, as this information will play a role in where the bedroom will be in the floor plan (especially if you are building from your own plans) and which family member gets which bedroom.

A bedroom may serve more than one purpose, but its first duty is to offer a place for catching the proverbial forty *undisturbed* winks. A quiet room starts with intelligent architectural planning. As we mentioned earlier, the layout of the house is important. If you're planning to build or remodel, place bedrooms on the inside of the house, away from the street, and set them apart from high-traffic areas such family rooms, dens, and the kitchen.

Traffic isn't the only problem. The best plans place bedrooms on the side of the house opposite the kitchen because odors of cooking food can disturb a deep slumber. We recall the Thanksgiving eve (before microwave ovens) when we decided to place a huge frozen turkey in the oven about midnight in order to make sure that it would be well done

CHAPTER 11

The Bedroom

and ready to serve for an early lunch the next afternoon. A separate bedroom wing (and a more powerful ventilation system) would have saved us from a sleepless night. That turkey was delicious, but as long as we lived in that house, we never placed another turkey in our oven on Thanksgiving eve.

Soundproofing

A comfortable bedroom is quiet. Materials make a big difference in the acoustical performance of both exterior and interior walls. Before you build or remodel, consider your choices. Brick and stone are better sound barriers than wood. Brick is more costly building material than wood clapboard or shakes, but if your new home is on a busy street, then it might be a wise investment.

Doubling interior walls helps soundproof rooms, but it is also expensive. A less expensive solution is to stagger studs that transmit sound so that alternate studs come in contact with the finished wall. Fiberglass insulation should be applied horizontally.

Consider making some modifications to keep bedrooms quiet. Floors and ceilings need special sound buffers when there are floors above or below. Floors should have insulation batts laid between joists. Then, subfloors should be installed, along with half-inch insulation boards and the surface flooring. If yours is a second-floor bedroom, placing carpeting or an area rug over a thick pad will muffle footsteps.

Ceilings are usually made of a hard surface material that bounces back sound waves, which actually amplifies them. Wood does this, and so do stone and tiles. These materials make singing in the bath satisfying but sleep almost impossible. If sleep is your number-one objective, consider an acoustical tile ceiling. Armstrong, the leading manufacturer of acoustical ceilings, has created some very attractively designed acoustical ceilings that look like wood planks. Beware of the ceilings that look like acoustical tile but have no sound-deadening qualities. Not all acoustical tiles are created equally. The sound-absorbing qualities of some are greater than others. Check the manufacturer's specifications on the packaging to make sure that you are getting the level of performance that you want.

If you decide that you want the benefits but not the appearance of acoustical tile, look into Novawall, a soundproofing system often used in corporate conference rooms, theaters, and private at-home sound studios by entertainment industry executives. Another alternative is to disguise acoustical tile ceilings with fabric tenting.

Doors made of solid wood block more sound than their hollow-core counterparts. You can also have your builder or remodeler build a soundproof door that sandwiches a panel of Acoustilead (a lead shield) between hardwood surfaces. Trims to block any cracks between the door and door frame also prevent transmission of sound. Your local home improvement store will carry both Acoustilead and trim.

Windows are very poor sound barriers. Installing double or triple thermopane windows (which have a vacuum between panes) are better sound deadeners than single-pane windows. Glass block, which lets in light but obscures the view, does an even better job of blocking sound. If it is light rather than the view that is important, glass block is an alternative.

If your home is older, you may not be able to change exterior materials of your house or change the partitioning walls. Changing the windows, however, may be the solution to the noise problem. Installing new windows is not necessarily costly or time-consuming. There are hundreds of national, local, and regional window manufacturers making replacement windows. A little investigation will help you discover the right ones for your bedroom. In New York City, where the roar of traffic can disturb sleep, apartment dwellers also cover their thermopane windows with another sheet of stationary glass.

Silent Surfaces

Once all that building and remodeling is done, you can turn your attention to interior surfaces. Even if you have done your best to build in quiet, there are still things that you can do to make your room conducive to sleep.

Walls are the largest surface area and most likely means of sound transmission. There are a few decorative solutions that function to dampen noise and increase the beauty of a room. Additional layers of sound-absorbing materials can reduce unpleasant reverberations within the room, a plus for watching television or listening to music.

Upholstered walls are more than merely the whim of a decorator. Fabric (especially thick velvet, tapestry, leather, or generously gathered thinner fabric) applied over a thick layer of padding blocks sound from entering, absorbs sounds from within the room, and provides a sense of unparalleled luxury.

There are a number of ways to upholster your walls. One way is to staple the fabric directly to walls with a staple gun. If you wish to take the fabric down at some point, you can also affix the fabric to strips of wood that are then nailed into the wall. Another method is to simply gather the fabric over rods and attach the rods to the wall with brackets. There are kits available at home decoration centers for do-it-yourself installation, or you may want to hire a professional. Interior designers can get the job done for you as can upholstery and drapery shops.

Other kinds of wall coverings also help muffle sound. Applying laminated heavy-weight fabric to walls works. Wallpaper, on the other hand, which is usually a hard, slick surface, does not. Stick to dense materials for the most effective sound absorption.

Undraped windows may be nice in the country; but, in town, use thick, heavy, lined and insulated floor-to-ceiling draperies. They do more than just add decorative grace notes. They are great sound and light barriers. They also establish a distinctive and luxurious mood, imparting a feeling of protection that creates well-being. For more about noise control, refer to chapter four.

Light Control

If you like to sleep late or work nights and sleep days, shutting out daylight may be essential to your well-being. Use blackout shades or blinds in addition to curtains and other window treatments. If you have window blinds that admit light at the sides, install a light-blocking frame made of one-inch by two-inch trim or picture frame molding inside the window sash. Keep in mind your need for light control if you are considering installing exotically shaped windows. Some are a challenge to cover with functional blinds, even with a custom window treatment.

Another solution, if you live in a tropical climate, is to install electrically operated hurricane shutters that can be lowered as needed. They also increase the security of your home.

Temperature Control

If you keep your bedroom hotter or cooler than the public areas of your home, make sure that it has its own thermostat, if possible. It is easy and inexpensive to create a two-zone (or more) plan for a new or remodeled house. Consider zoning bedrooms according to the needs of the occupants. A two-zone or multiple-zone system will conserve electrical consumption and provide you with comfortable temperatures year round.

Lighting

In the bedroom, planned lighting is a safety and convenience measure. An easy-to-manipulate, wrist-high rocker switch at the bedroom door for overall room illumination is a sensible way to prevent a fall. A night light that turns on automatically is recommended. If you are building or remodeling, the convenience of light control from the bedside is a must. Don't take for granted that the electrician will automatically add that feature. Remember to ask for the specific features you want. The additional convenience of better and additional switches is worth a few extra dollars.

Bedtime reading is not just for kids. A good reading light in the bedroom is a must for almost everyone. Where to place lighting is a personal choice. You or your partner may prefer a straight-backed chair, table, or desk and table lamp with a halogen bulb for more serious reading. For those who like to read in bed, propped up by plump pillows, a wall-hung adjustable light with a halogen bulb that can be readjusted whenever you shift to a new, more comfortable position is the most convenient lighting choice. Install one on each side of the bed. This type of lamp is more effective at providing glare-free light than table lamps, which never seem to shield eyes properly from the bulb.

Some bedrooms are roomy enough for a grouping of an easy chair, lamp, and table with a shelf or drawer for people who like serious reading. For bedrooms where space is limited, a comfortable chair or recliner and a pole lamp with an attached small round glass shelf is a good substitute. As for reading chairs, Lexington, Ralph Lauren, and other manufacturers are creating chairs with book pockets attached to the arms and backs or shelves below the seats for stashing your favorite reading material.

Beds

Since we each have our own comfort criteria, the first step in selecting a bed is to decide what important comfort issues you need to solve. Beds must do more than simply provide a place to lie down. If that were the case, there would not be the hundreds of styles of beds available today. Some bed styles feature important pluses that save space. Others solve decorative problems. To simplify a complex decision, determine first which type of bed suits your lifestyle and your decorating scheme.

Storage

Bedrooms in most American homes are about ten feet by twelve feet. That's not exactly huge. Add the fact that the entry door, closet doors, and perhaps a bathroom door subtracts from wall space, and you often have a problem of where to place the bed. In some of these cases, there is not enough space for bedside tables, even though you need somewhere to store an alarm clock, radio, TV control, the book you are reading, and other stuff.

Consider the problems posed by a small guest bedroom. Each one of the four walls had an awkwardly placed door or window so that there was no wall area wide enough to place the bed and two bedside tables needed for lamps and general convenience. There were also no light fixtures accessible, which forced guests to crawl across the bed or walk around it while hoping they wouldn't stumble over a suitcase.

A better solution would have been a bookcase headboard for storage space that would have added only ten to twelve inches to the length of

the bed, leaving adequate walk-around space. Hanging wall lamps could have provided illumination for reading in bed. A floor lamp could provide light at the entry.

Other Storage Problems

Storing extra quilts and blankets is a problem in many bedrooms. A captain's bed, designed like the ones for ships, provides a drawer beneath the mattress for storage. These beds are not just for sailors, nor are they strictly for children and teenagers. Captain's beds are available in most sizes (except perhaps king sizes) and in a variety of styles, including the most popular, Campaign, whose style was inspired by Napoleon.

Capturing a View

A raised bed can place a magnificent view at eye level. To take advantage of a spectacular sight of both the ocean and the waterway from a higher-than-average four-poster bed was one woman's solution. Watching the changing hues of the ocean and boats was her soothing comfort and delightful distraction.

Four-poster beds are generally based on some historic period or style. If none suits your taste or decorating scheme, consider the contemporary solution of the platform bed, a design idea taken from platforms that elevated the beds of European kings who held court in their bedrooms. Plan the platform as you would stairs, using the same criteria; that is, easy-to-maneuver risers, ideally about seven and a half inches high with twelve-inch- to fifteen-inch-wide treads. If the platform is more than one step high, include a decorative but easy-to-grasp handrail. We recognize the need for a handrail for a stairway, but one or two steps can be disarmingly dangerous. Often, we don't take them seriously.

An important comfort factor for a platform or any other built-in bed is that the base should be recessed, leaving an eight-inch toe kick area similar to that beneath kitchen cabinets. Stubbed toes hurt! Any sort of high wood side support on platform, captain's, and rustic beds should be lower than the top of the mattress to prevent hurting your knee as you crawl into bed.

Guest Beds

A guest bed for occasional sleep-overs is an important extra in a child's room. A trundle bed that neatly stores a second bed beneath it is the ideal solution for children's rooms and for guest rooms. The Murphy bed, a concealed bed that is stored in a wall cabinet, is the perfect solution for rooms that do double duty as guest rooms and dens, libraries, and home offices. Upholstered beds, a true decorator's delight, double as sofas, and are also a good option in a home office or other double-duty room. Convertible sofa beds have not been critically acclaimed for comfort, but manufacturers continue to make improvements. For any bed, magic finger foam pads give an extra dollop of comfort.

And So, to Sleep

A key to comfort is finding a mattress to meet our unique needs. How do we select the right one? Innerspring mattresses—tempered spring coils covered by layers of upholstery—are the most popular. The best queen size (the most popular size) mattress is made with more than 375 tempered steel coils and several layers of upholstery. Some also have one or more layers of foam and a quilted pillow top.

Some manufacturers encourage you to design your own mattress. You can order a customized mattress that has exactly the number and kind of layers of materials that you deem most comfortable. While you are at it, order a matching box spring. Innerspring mattresses come paired with box springs designed to work together. Experts advise against combining a new mattress with old box springs. If you order a custom mattress, be prepared to order custom sheets to fit.

An alternative to the innerspring is the foam mattress. A foundation or box spring is also needed for a foam mattress. Foam density should measure at least two pounds per cubic foot. The higher the density, the better the foam.

Water beds offer yet another choice. You can select a soft-side style that looks like an innerspring. Inside an upholstered cover is a vinyl covering over easy-to-fill cylinders. The vinyl should be at least twenty millimeters thick. The hard-side model has a vinyl mattress, liner, and heater encased in a wooden frame. You'll need special sheets for this model. Water beds have wave motions ranging from waveless to full flotation. Be sure to try a waterbed to make sure its degree of motion is for you.

Futons, another choice usually reserved for the occasional guest, are made of layers of cotton batting with perhaps a core layer of foam, encased in cotton ticking. Some models are stored as sofas by a frame that supports the futon.

There seems to be no substitute for testing a potential purchase by following Goldilocks's example; that is, actually lying down on the mattress you are considering purchasing. Lying down in the store may seem undignified, but it is the only way to find out if the mattress works for you. There is no objective standard for judging and labeling firmness. The quality of firmness varies from make to make, so that you cannot rely on a label. You and your body are the only real judges. It will take several minutes of resting on the mattress. Wear comfortable clothing and get into the positions you actually sleep in.

You'll also need to know whether the mattress is long enough to suit your comfort needs. The bed should be six inches longer than the height of the tallest person sleeping in the bed. A six-foot person measures seventy-two inches. Mattresses vary in length from seventy-five to eighty inches. Standard sizes are: twin (thirty-nine by seventy-five inches), full or double (fifty-four by seventy-five inches), queen (sixty by eighty inches) and king (seventy-six by eighty inches). Extra-long twin and full mattresses are eighty inches long. Custom beds can be made for exceptionally tall people and for uniquely sized bed frames.

Bedding

Cotton or linen sheets absorb moisture and are pleasant to the touch. For most of us, these are the most comfortable sheets. Synthetic fibers are often blended with natural fibers in less expensive sheets. In addition to helping keep manufacturing costs down, synthetic fibers help reduce wrinkling.

If you or householders are troubled by allergies, use white sheets with a high thread count that can be washed in hot water to reduce dust mites. If your budget allows, buy at least two sets so that you are never stuck with an unmade bed. All bedding materials should be washable. Be sure to buy dust ruffles to cover the bed frame and box springs. An additional fitted sheet can be used to cover the box spring if a dust ruffle is not used.

Arranging Your Room

Ideally, there should be a night table on either side of the bed. The standard nightstand size is roughly twenty by twenty-four inches—barely enough space for a lamp. This is all the more reason to forgo table lamps for the wall-hung type that leave tabletops free for a telephone, clock radio, and basic supplies. If space permits, a larger table will offer more surface for placing things that add to personal comfort. If it is much larger, attach easy-to-roll casters so that you can push the table away when you're ready to make the bed. Also, make sure the bed is on casters and can be easily moved for cleaning. Regular cleaning under the bed will control dust and dust mites.

Placing a bed parallel to the wall saves floor space. A *lit close* is the French name for draped beds placed in niches. A table on casters works well with such a bed because it is easily moved when the bed is made. Recessed shelves at either end of a niche augment or replace the bedside table.

Since the bed is the most important piece of furniture in the bedroom, the rule is that the headboard should be opposite the entry door so that it serves as the natural focal point of the room. That is not always possible, of course. A more helpful guideline is that the bed should not obstruct a door or passage through the room. Psychologically, we are rebuffed by barriers of this sort and it is awkward and inefficient to have to walk around a bed to get to a closet or the bathroom.

Be flexible in considering what some will view as unorthodox arrangements. It doesn't cost much in time and energy to experiment with a new arrangement. Olga Kenniburg's small bedroom in an apartment on Chicago's Lakeshore Drive was redesigned using furniture she disliked because she thought it made the room unattractive. Thinking the furniture falsely accused (it was just in the wrong place), we removed a double dresser from its place in the corner against a window wall and repositioned it in the middle of the room with its finished back against the end of a canopy bed. We removed a mirror and rehung it over the headboard. We placed a small TV atop the dresser. The owner could then lie in bed, watch TV, and see the front of the now handsome dresser reflected in a floor-to-ceiling mirrored wall. A chaise lounge fit where the dresser had formerly stood. The canopied bed, chaise lounge, and window draperies were made of pink sheets bought at a white sale from nearby Marshall Fields. This room's new look cost very little. The room, because of its unbeatable combination of economy and good looks, was featured in *Parade* and two other magazines.

An old rule is to never place a headboard in front of a window. There are a number of practical reasons why this might not be the best placement, including drafts and risks from falling glass in case the window breaks during a storm or earthquake. Traditionally, a bed is placed in a sheltered, protected location. A bed might look dramatic placed in front of an interesting window with an exciting window treatment, but you will want to make sure first that the risks and discomforts are minimal. Window areas are reserved for desks, vanities, or other pieces of furniture that require an abundance of natural light.

Placing a bed on the diagonal was once a decorating taboo. Now it is a convention that makes a room seem more dynamic, improves passage, and gains access to a spectacular view or rare summer breezes. *If it feels good, do it.* This is a legitimate maxim where personal comfort is the goal.

Storage in the Bedroom

Simple, shallow closets in the master bedroom are old-fashioned. They're being replaced with oversized, walk-in, his-and-her dressing closets. New California closets—closets outfitted with wire shelving systems—free floor space from dressers and chests of drawers. In their stead, a writing desk or small table and chairs for snacks help transform a bedroom into a real master suite. Sometimes it is possible to kill two birds with one stone—gain floor space and outfit a closet inexpensively—by getting the double dresser or chest of drawers out of the bedroom and into a walk-in closet. This was the case for one homeowner who loved the storage capacity of her Early American dresser that looked so right in New Jersey but so wrong in Florida.

Bed and Bath Trends

The master suite, a standard element in new homes in the '80s, proved so luxurious, efficient, and convenient that homeowners took the concept one step farther in the '90s by adding his-and-her baths and dressing areas. Builders and homeowners now are introducing the same time- and energy-saving bed and bath combinations to other bedrooms. If the budget is tight, Jack-and-Jill baths placed between children's bedrooms are a convenient solution.

Most of us are not looking for the ultimate in sybaritic creature comforts but will be grateful for basic conveniences that are sometimes overlooked even in newly built or remodeled houses. After spending $50,000 dollars to renovate the master bedroom suite's bath, there was not any kind of quick heat source for those below-zero winter work-week mornings when no one could wait forty-five minutes for the central furnace to heat the room. One entire wall had no electrical outlets. Adding heat lamps and outlets after the fact was too expensive. The solution: an extension cord and an electric heater placed far away from water and other dangers, until the owners could install a heater in the toekick space in the vanity cabinet.

The design process for the comfortable bedroom begins with defining the design problem. Creating the most convenient environment for resting and grooming is half the problem, the other half is meeting all (or most) of your requirements. To design the comfortable bedroom, take inventory of your needs. The checklist below will help you pull together some crucial information about the furnishings that are essential to your lifestyle needs. Because comfort is so individual, a checklist should be completed for each bedroom user.

The Bedroom Checklist

Who will occupy the bedroom? What is the personal style preference of the occupant?

❑ Master bedroom suite _____
❑ Casual
❑ Sophisticated
❑ Whimsical
❑ Bedroom 1 _____
❑ Casual
❑ Sophisticated
❑ Whimsical
❑ Bedroom 2 _____
❑ Casual
❑ Sophisticated
❑ Whimsical
❑ Bedroom 3 _____
❑ Casual
❑ Sophisticated
❑ Whimsical

What functions will the bedrooms serve?

❑ Sleeping
❑ Resting/sleeping by day
❑ Reading
❑ Study/homework
❑ Television viewing
❑ Guest room
❑ Sleep-overs

- ❑ Grooming/makeup
- ❑ Intimate conversation area
- ❑ Play space
- ❑ Stereo/music
- ❑ Convalescence
- ❑ Hangout space for teens
- ❑ Hobby
- ❑ Other _____

What furnishings are needed in each room?

- ❑ Bed _____
- ❑ Nightstands
- ❑ Occasional tables
- ❑ Sofa/love seat
- ❑ Easy chair
- ❑ Lounge chair
- ❑ Chaise lounge
- ❑ Convertible sofa bed
- ❑ Futon
- ❑ Vanity
- ❑ Hope chest
- ❑ Desk
- ❑ Chair (for study/work)
- ❑ Built-in storage/desk
- ❑ Armoire
- ❑ Bureau/chest of drawers
- ❑ Footlocker
- ❑ Mirrors
- ❑ Media cabinet

What equipment is needed for each room?

- ❑ Television
- ❑ VCR
- ❑ Computer
- ❑ Stereo
- ❑ Intercom
- ❑ Telephone
- ❑ Fax
- ❑ Answering machine
- ❑ Private telephone line

What storage facilities are needed?

- ❑ Cabinets
- ❑ Open shelves
- ❑ Drawers
- ❑ Closets
- ❑ Walk-in closets (number of closets) _____

How much hanging storage is needed? (Measure in linear feet.)

- ❑ Pants _____
- ❑ Skirts _____
- ❑ Suits _____
- ❑ Shirts/blouses _____
- ❑ Dresses _____
- ❑ Coats _____

How much shelving space is required? (Measure height and width of folded garments.)

- ❑ _____

How many linear feet of drawers is needed for . . . ?

- ❑ Shallow drawers _____
- ❑ Deep drawers _____

How many pairs of shoes? Where do you prefer storing them?

- ❏ _____
- ❏ Floor storage
- ❏ Wall-mounted
- ❏ Back of closet

Where is task lighting needed?

- ❏ At bedsides
- ❏ Tables
- ❏ Desk
- ❏ Vanity

CHAPTER 12

The Bath: Making a Comfortable Splash

The comfortable bath is one well adapted for the purpose of risk-free, easy use. It should be a pleasurable space that makes the early-morning rush seem effortless and nightly regimes soothing bedtime preludes. If you're building a new house, you have a wonderful opportunity to create a bath that suits many different moods. A well-planned bath will serve all your needs—from a quick morning eye-opening shower just as hot as you like it, to a leisurely midnight soak. If you're not planning to build, consider remodeling the uncomfortable bath you're living with. Layering on lush decorative accessories may make the room seem cozier, but it cannot change a poor layout, compensate for outmoded fixtures, or make the room any more functional. Without architectural bones, purely cosmetic decorative comforts are unsatisfying over the long run.

Because more is expected from today's baths, upgrading an older bath will add real value to a home. According to a nationwide survey of real estate agents in 1995, a well-remodeled bath brought about an 85 percent return on investment. A modern bath is essential for resale (according to many real estate agents), especially in areas where sales are competitive.

Expensive materials do not ensure a great bath. Excellent planning is the key to achieving a wonderful, truly useful bath. Whether you're building a new bath or updating an older one, smart planning will help you control costs by avoiding delays in deliveries of supplies and materials, expensive tear-outs and redos, and other budget-crunching mistakes. To make good design easier to recognize and simpler to achieve, the National Kitchen and Bath Association has devised a new set of design rules that explain exactly how to get the most from your new bath. Knowing these rules, which appear on pages 156–157, will make it easier to communicate your ideas to architects and builders.

In the past, creating a great bath was more art than science, accident than intent. There was no single authority or guide for spatial planning and the nearest thing to guidelines were criteria developed by the Department of Housing and Urban Development in the 1950s. Certain industry standards such as the thirty-two-inch-high vanity (a concept that's not yet entirely dead) cannot be traced to any responsible source. Yet, until recently, manufacturers have been building these low, back-breaking vanities. The rules by which baths were constructed in previous decades seemed based on arbitrary measurements more suitable to the builder's than the homeowner's needs. This probably explains why baths in many older homes are claustrophobically tiny, as well as inconveniently planned. In the high-flying '80s, affluent homeowners set a trend for the Great Bath that was, in some cases, as big as the master bedroom.

That was then. The idea of luxury in the '90s is incorporating more baths into the home. When families must choose between one big bath or two small ones, two baths win hands down. Michigan homeowners won a national magazine's 1995 bathroom remodeling contest by cleverly building two full baths where one six-feet by thirteen-feet bath had been. Their new master bath, only four feet by eight feet, has a shower, toilet, and lavatory—all the fixtures necessary for a full bath. Thanks to excellent planning, there's ample walk-around room so this small room seems gracious, not cramped.

Why are there new bath design rules at this stage of the bathroom design game? Professional designers noticed that old rules, mainly conventions that had evolved over time, were no longer relevant to the way we live today. They saw that Europeans were using higher vanities and pedestal sinks that require less bending and put less strain on the back, and that certain ergonomic studies, initially conducted to aid designs for tight space capsules, offered benefits not just to astronauts but to the whole population.

The Elements of Comfortable, Convenient Bath Design

The first step in planning an accommodating bathroom is determining the layout or physical placement of fixtures, taking into account architectural elements such as windows and doors that affect fixture placement. More than half of the new design rules deal with spatial requirements for the comfortable use and cleaning of fixtures. Smart layout planning not only makes the best possible use of available space, it also helps save on plumbing costs.

If you're remodeling, leaving the toilet in its existing place can save as much as $300 in plumbing costs. If doing this is possible, next see if you can rearrange the space without roughing in any new water, waste, and vent lines (another savings). You can offset the toilet waste line only two inches and still turn the toilet in a different direction that's much more convenient. You can offset the water and waste lines by as much as twelve inches, which could allow you to relocate the lavatory inside a vanity cabinet. If a cabinet is crowding the toilet so that it's impossible to stand between the two (which was the case in a New Jersey bath we redesigned), cut costs by exchanging the misery-making vanity with a corner or pedestal sink.

To save time (yours and/or an expensive plumber's) and dollars, use the fewest fixtures design principle. The only fixtures you need for a tiny, fully functional bath are a toilet, lavatory, and shower. You can do without a tub, which takes up a disproportionate amount of limited space. If you must have a whirlpool tub, but only have an average-sized bathroom, use what is known as a *replacement whirlpool* in a standard tub size.

For great layout flexibility, consider small-scale fixtures or corner fixtures. Additional floor space afforded by these fixtures eliminates that crowded feeling and makes blow-drying hair, applying makeup, or dressing possible. Furthermore, many powder rooms may, on close scrutiny, reveal adequate space for an asymmetrical or neo-angle shower.

Safety in the bath is a growing concern. Many of the new design rules concern safety issues. Especially worth noting is the safe-stair rule that calls for only one step leading to a tub. It's surprising how many pictures of whirlpool tubs raised above floor level and surrounded by flights of slippery marble stairs one sees in decorating and remodeling magazines. Add handrails to whirlpool tubs, whether they're raised above or sunken below floor level. Steps with ten-inch-deep treads and seven and one-quarter-inch risers are more easily and safely negotiated than the industry standard nine-inch-wide tread and eight and one-quarter-inch-high riser.

Another important safety feature addressed by the new rules is that a shower door should swing into the bathroom. This simple precaution allows easy rescue of anyone injured or incapacitated while showering.

A third important rule states that shower heads must be protected by pressure-balance temperature regulators or temperature-limiting devices. This rule results from concern for the staggering number of accidental scaldings of children in baths—37,000 per year were reported by the National Safe Kids Campaign.

Lighting is both a safety and convenience factor in the bath. A tub/shower light may be optional with some, but the new rules state that every bath should have a moisture-proof shower/tub light as well as adequate general and task lighting. Lighting increases visibility and safety, particularly if a shower curtain will be used.

Storage is high on the list of important features home buyers look for in baths. The new *convenient storage rule* says that supplies such as toilet paper, soap, and towels should be within reach of the user.

Mechanical ventilation is a new rule. Do not count on windows or skylights to take away unpleasant odors and potentially damaging moisture. Ventilators equipped with automatic sensors and timers will ensure that excess moisture is vented out. Water left behind by showers and baths encourages unsightly and unhealthy mold and mildew buildup. Providing for adequate ventilation will preserve tile grout.

The appearance of your new bath depends on personal taste and falls into the realm of *decorating*, rather than space planning, so style is strictly up to you. However, if you're redoing a bath with resale in mind, furnish it with up-to-date, low-maintenance materials in easy-to-live-with neutral colors that are popular with most of today's home buyers. According to realtors surveyed by a leading building trade magazine, these include solid-surface vanity counters with molded sinks, new lighting, mirrored medicine cabinets, and ceramic tile floor and walls in the tub/shower area. (Vinyl wall covering is acceptable for the rest of the room.) Neutral-colored fixtures allow future owners to add their own favorite colors in wall coverings.

If you are in the early stages of planning your comfortable bath, consider these budget-stretching design tips:

1. Use white fixtures—they cost less than colored ones.
2. Chrome fittings and accessories are less expensive than brass.
3. Vinyl flooring is less costly than ceramic tile, which has greater resale appeal.
4. If you use ceramic tile, avoid expensive decorator tiles. Instead, create designs with a variety of inexpensive plain tiles.
5. Use bigger ceramic tiles for walls (eight inches by ten inches) and floors (twelve inches by twelve inches): They look fine even in a small bath and are less expensive to install than smaller tiles with more grout lines because they require less installation time and maintenance.
6. To protect your investment of money, time, and effort in a new bath, plan on using a cement gypsum tile backer board behind the shower and tub. An ounce of prevention is worth at least a pound of cure when it comes to water-damaged interior bathroom walls.

The National Kitchen and Bath Association's Bath Design Rules

These NKBA design rules address issues of workable and usable space, safety, comfort, and convenience.

Workable Space

1. Make the entrance a thirty-two-inch-wide clear walkway.
2. Provide at least six inches between fixtures for cleaning ease.
3. Leave twenty-one inches of clear walkway space in front of the lavatory.
4. Leave twenty-one inches of clear walkway space in front of the toilet.
5. Leave a fifteen-inch minimum clearance from the lavatory centerline to a side wall.
6. Leave a thirty-inch minimum clearance between two bowls in the lavatory countertop.
7. Provide a fifteen-inch minimum clearance from the center of the toilet to any obstruction, fixture, or equipment on either side.
8. Install the toilet paper holder within reach of one seated on the toilet (slightly in front of the edge of the toilet bowl, centered twenty-six inches above the finished floor).
9. The minimum size for a usable shower is thirty-two inches by thirty-two inches.
10. A minimum walkway in front of the tub/shower is twenty-one inches.

Safety-First Features

1. Make sure that no doors interfere with fixtures.
2. All receptacles must have ground fault circuit interrupters. No switch may be within sixty inches of a water source. Use a moisture-proof, special-purpose light fixture above tub or shower units.

3. Only one step should lead to the tub, and that step must be at least ten inches deep and not more than seven and a quarter inches high.
4. Bathtub faucets must be accessible from outside the tub.
5. Provide at least one grab bar to facilitate bathtub or shower entry.
6. Install a bench within the shower enclosure.
7. The shower door should swing into the bathroom.
8. Protect shower heads by installing a pressure-balance/temperature regulator or temperature-limiting device.
9. Use slip-resistant flooring.

Convenience and Comfort Factors
1. A mechanical ventilation system is mandatory.
2. If the bathroom has a bidet, store soap and towels within reach.
3. Provide whirlpool motor access.
4. Include a counter or shelf around the lavatory, space for grooming equipment, a shampoo and soap shelf in the shower and/or tub, and hanging space for linens.
5. Provide adequate heat.
6. Provide adequate general and task lighting.

Luxury: Comfort Beyond Design Guidelines

The NKBA guidelines are intended to assure basic comforts in standard-sized bathrooms (approximately five feet by nine feet). If you've got the space and ingenuity, expect your designs to go beyond the guidelines in your pursuit of greater comfort and convenience. For example, you may have enough room to place one or more toilets behind closed doors or in a niche with a privacy screen. When we were asked to create a master bath in a 1920s home in the Northeast, a small room next door to the master bedroom, originally intended as a dressing room or nursery, proved the perfect place. An adjacent hall closet presented us with a choice: use it as a linen closet or a niche for the toilet. The wife decided that a large wall-hung kitchen cabinet matching the cabinets used for the vanity would serve adequately for linens, so the former hall closet was incorporated into the bathroom and the toilet was installed there. To provide even greater privacy for the niche, she devised a thirty-two-inch-high freestanding folding screen by hinging together three louvered shutters.

Just as his and her lavatories are more efficient and comfortable than a single lavatory, his and her vanities are even more convenient. If space and budget allow, why not?

Perhaps you would like to incorporate a steam bath in its own special corner, while the whirlpool occupies another, a shower in its own spot, and a standard tub in yet another. Before calling a plumber, use the NKBA design guidelines to experiment with a variety of possible layouts. Draw your room to scale on graph paper, complete with windows, doors, and other architectural features. Make several copies so that you can rough in a number of layout possibilities until you find one that seems best for you. Close your eyes and take a mental walk through the space as you've arranged it. Try to see the space as you move from place to place in your mind's eye. Imagine opening and closing doors and drawers. Is there enough room for drawers in opposing cabinets to open? Do drawers collide with a fixture or with one another? When drawers or doors are open, is there enough space for you to stand or for two people to walk around? This paper scenario can save dollars and prevent tears. It's worth the exercise.

Fabulous Faucets, Fixtures, and Furnishings

Nothing will have more to do with your comfort in the bath than faucets and fixtures that work well. Buy the very best that you can afford. That doesn't mean that you have to break the bank to pay for a European brand faucet that is listed at $495. American manufacturers such as Jado and Moen, for example, make high-quality washerless, ceramic disk, no-leak faucets with easy-to-maneuver lever handles for under $200. Look for solid brass or stainless steel faucets for long life. If you must sacrifice or make budgetary shortcuts, there are other, better ways to do it than buying cheap fixtures. You'll only have to replace them sooner than you'd like.

Today, faucets have many comfort features that were simply not available a few years ago. Like the old models, they turn the water flow off and on, but the new models are safer and easier to use than the old-fashioned ones. Safety concerns have led to new safety stops that prevent a user from turning a faucet to a harmfully high temperature. It's simple to install a device such as this to prevent accidental scalding even on older faucets. These devices are inexpensive. Ergonomically designed faucets are easier to grasp and maneuver. Those designed for greater accessibility do not have to be tightly grasped. They can be operated with five pounds or less of force. Handy pull-out spray faucets are not only for kitchens anymore. In the bathroom, they make shampooing easier and more comfortable. Push-button controls on the handle make them easy to control. Some come with vacuum breaker valves (just like kitchen faucets) that prevent unhealthy backflow of water from the sink. Some have extra-long hoses that make tasks easier.

If you're impatient and waiting makes you uncomfortable, be sure that the faucet you choose for your whirlpool tub is a fast-fill type that fills no slower than the rate of twenty-three gallons per minute at forty psi of water pressure.

Showerheads offer more options for various types of water delivery than ever before. Kohler (with its new MasterShower and SuperShower Towers) led the way in providing multiple restricted-flow showerheads that let you indulge in water flowing from many different directions that conserve at the same time. Low-flow water heads are mandated by code in most regions. The challenge for engineers has been to comply but still deliver a shower spray that invigorates or relaxes. Grohe makes a multihead shower system that combines an overhead showerhead, hand-held showers, and body sprays. This system, like many others today, works with a thermostatic value to ensure limitless comfort and no accidental scaldings. Pressure-balance valves, which work differently, also are designed to prevent surprise hot water (or cold water) surges. It's easy to see why every shower should have one.

Showerheads, for greatest comfort, should be at a comfortable height. If you share a shower with someone appreciably taller or shorter, it might make more sense (and be a great deal more comfortable) to install a showerhead for each.

Showers are great energizers and aids to relaxation. If you'd like to jump-start your day, try a cool shower that narrows the blood vessels and activates the circulatory system. You'll be stimulated to action. A hot shower widens blood vessels and relaxes the muscles for a calming effect—the perfect evening antidote to a stressful day. There are so many types of showers. Which one's for you?

First of all, shower stalls don't have to be huge. Generally, they can be as small as thirty-six inches square, but in some cases we've successfully created smaller ones. In a Summit, New Jersey, house, we carved enough space from an adjoining dining room to create a twenty-four-inch by thirty-six-inch-wide shower that turned a hall powder room into a full bath. Other designers have turned side-by-side closets between bedrooms into a Jack-and-Jill bath that serves both bedrooms.

Neo-angle (asymmetrical) showers, especially those with glass walls and doors, make smart use of oddly angled spaces in small rooms. Transparent glass shower doors and walls make these tight rooms seem larger and infinitely glamorous. Expect to pay more for frameless doors (the starting price is $200). You'll pay a lot more for a custom glass enclosure (walls and doors) which is tailor made for a particular space ($1,500 and up), but these beautiful and ultimately practical showers offer unsurpassed comfort.

Tubs should be wide enough to use. Recently, we inspected a house in Florida for a prospective buyer. One of the first things we noticed was that the master bath's tub was undersized. The buyer is not. If he buys the house, he'll have to replace the tub. Tubs no longer have to be bone-crushingly hard. There's at least one soft standard bathtub on the market. If you haven't seen it, investigate. Called the SoftTub, this tub has an outside surface that is rigid enough to hold water but soft enough that you won't bruise your knee if you lean against the edge as you climb in. And as for climbing, a tub shouldn't be too high. Kohler makes a tub with a door in the side and a seat at one end.

When it comes to tubs, whirlpools are in a league of their own. They started life as therapeutic aids in hospitals. They did their job well. Even able-bodied people discovered their benefits and soon whirlpool tubs were builder's extras or custom items. Now, they're standard in almost every new home because they're a great boon to those who need and want their restorative benefits. How do you assess the comfort and convenience of a whirlpool tub? Frankly, you may not find an ideally comfortable whirlpool. Why? Because large-scale tubs are so deep (eighteen to twenty inches) that they must be sunken or enthroned. Low or high, they're reachable only via a row of intimidating, slippery, stone steps. Few have a handrail. The best we can do to make existing models more comfortable is insist on one with a seatlike ledge and a rail that we can grasp as we sit and swing ourselves safely into the tub.

If your small bathroom has only space for the existing standard tub, you don't have to deny yourself the comforts of a whirlpool bath. Most manufacturers make a sixty-inch-long whirlpool tub that can replace a standard tub. They're heavier, of course, so you may need to shore up the floor. Fortunately, some whirlpool tubs are lighter in weight than others. Americast by American Standard, for example, is a material that looks like cast iron but weighs only half as much. For greatest comfort, select a model with jets placed where you need them. Regardless of the number of jets you choose (models include two to eight jets), make sure that they're multidirectional. Other comfort features include grab bars, seats, headrests and footrests, in-line heaters to maintain a steady water temperature, mood lights, and electronic controls.

Large, luxurious bathrooms offer a great many comforts, but even the most basic bathroom takes comfortable care of your basic needs. No matter how small the space, there's almost no excuse for not having a comfortable, well-functioning bathroom. Corner fixtures—vanities, showers, and even toilets—come to the rescue. They save space without sacrificing good looks or the safety and convenience features found on standard models.

You'll also find convenience features on fixtures that are deliberately designed to save water; low-flush, pressure-assisted or gravity-fed toilets, faucets that conform to the 2.5 gpm (gallons per minute) standard, 2.2

gpm showerheads, pressure balancing tub/shower valves that meet low-flow standards, and more.

As you can tell, manufacturers are working overtime to make everything about the bath safer, more socially responsive, more personally comfortable, and more beautiful, too.

A Word About Bathroom Windows

Windows and skylights aid but cannot substitute for ventilation, which you will need to draw away moisture and thus prevent mildew in your bath, steam room, sauna, or exercise room. It's our obsession with natural light and our delight in beautiful views that make windows just as important in the bath as in other rooms. However, not all of us have enchanted gardens or wonderful woodlands stretching for miles just outside our bathroom window, nor can we walk through one glass shower door and out another straight into the Pacific Ocean as do the owners of one California bathroom. Some of us have neighbors. In this case, big, translucent windows just won't do in our baths. That doesn't mean that we can't have natural light and lots of it. When we designed a bath in a house with a zero lot line in Boca Raton, Florida, the builder offered a choice between a large window or a skylight. A transparent window was out of the question. The small skylight created a meager puddle of light in the middle of the seventeen-feet-long room. That small pool of light did nothing to keep that room from looking distressingly narrow and gloomy. We substituted glass block for the large window. The effect of sunlight streaming through the opaque glass block was stunning. The room looked twice its size and seemed cheerful, welcoming, and very private.

In an older house in Washington, D.C., an architect friend decided there was really no better location for a new toilet than the spot the old one occupied—in front of a second-story window—so that's where he placed the new toilet. Since both natural light and privacy were musts, he had the existing windowpane sandblasted. To make the frosted pane more decorative, he created a pattern relating to one found in the carved wood molding. Now the window is attractive from inside and out.

Auxiliary Heat

It is often necessary to warm up the bathroom on frosty mornings before the central heat is turned on. Auxiliary heaters are available in a number of different styles. You can choose from an electric ceiling fixture with a blower, a fan-forced wall heater with its own thermostat, a kick-space heater, a ceiling unit with an infrared bulb and ventilation fan, or others. Towel warmers not only serve up toasty towels, they double as auxiliary heat sources. Freestanding heaters with dangling electric cords are dangerous in the bath. It's best to install your auxiliary heater. Why not put a fan-forced wall heater unit inside a small bench, with vents at the base? Place the bench near the lavatory and it can serve as a stool.

Finishing Touches

Little changes mean a lot when it comes to comfort. Light where you need it (in the shower, above the vanity, overall room illumination, wall sconces for dimming in the evening, and a night light) is a must and a gracious finishing touch. An antique dresser plumbed to serve as a vanity is another. So is a beautifully framed mirror in lieu of the garden-variety plate glass. One New York City dweller had no closet in the bath of her big, old brownstone. Space allowed her to choose between building in a closet or converting a large old armoire to a linen closet that held towels galore. She chose the armoire. It's perfectly functional, adds real style to her bath, and she can take it with her, should she move.

Electronic controls that preset your shower or bath and turn it on from your approaching car are certainly comfortable. So are timers that regulate your shower. Radios and televisions in the bath are comfort grace notes for media buffs. So is piped-in music.

One of the most helpful comforts we ever saw in a bath was a space-saving stacked washer and dryer. Imagine the luxury of having a washer and dryer just where you need it—where all those wet towels originate.

Sauna Stuff

Who needs the comforts of a sauna? Practically everyone who is under stress, according to a physician we interviewed for a magazine article. He and his wife, a nurse, take nightly saunas to manage stress. He enjoys the feeling of relaxation that the sauna's dry heat produces after vigorous exercise. He considers the sauna more effective than a sleeping pill.

Saunas are not out of reach in terms of cost, nor do you have to build on an addition to your house. Saunas for one or two come in prefabricated kits small enough to fit into an oversized closet. Kits for larger models are also available.

Most manufacturers say that the basement is a great place to install a sauna. With a manufacturer's easy-to-follow instructions, you can do it in as little as four hours. All you will need is a hammer and saw (to cut some pieces to fit). The electric sauna heater used to heat the sauna stones must be carefully installed. If you install your sauna in the basement, it won't be necessary to build a floor. A slatted wood mat covers the concrete floor. Never install a sauna over a carpeted floor, manufacturers warn. The wood mat lifts out for easy maintenance. Along with saunas, steam baths and exercise rooms are natural extensions of the bath. They're comfort features in today's upscale homes.

Like saunas, steam bath kits can be purchased. Installation is quick and easy. Exercise areas can range from a few pieces of equipment in the corner of the bedroom or bath to a whole room devoted to an array of machines. You can, of course, start with one or two pieces of exercise equipment and add on as you like. To enjoy exercise in comfort, you'll need a quiet, carpeted room to absorb noise and vibrations from the equipment, a pad or bench for resting, towels for mopping up all that sweat, and probably music to work by. Yes, exercise is work. We just want as comfortable a place in which to do it as our homes can afford.

Universal Baths

Not everyone is an able-bodied, young-to-middle-aged person. Certainly, none of us will be that forever, so we may want to plan ahead. For a new bath with the longest possible comfort life, add to the NKBA's new design rules these ideas for a universal bath. Universal design aims to make baths adaptable for easy use by all. A bath should be easy to negotiate and utilize, particularly for wheelchair or walker users and others who may have limited mobility.

Manual dexterity matters. A person seated in a wheelchair has a comfortable reach from twenty to twenty-four inches, or about fifty-four inches above the floor. Light, air-conditioning, heat, and security controls should be within a comfortable reach zone of fifteen to forty-two inches above floor level. Instead of small, hard-to-manipulate switches, use large buttons or pad controls. Lever handles are easier to grasp and operate than round knobs, so they are excellent choices for exterior and interior doors as well as for faucets for bathroom lavatories. Pull-out spray faucets with button controls on the handle are also easy to operate in the bath. These should retract easily when not in use.

Doorways can and should be enlarged to thirty-four to thirty-six inches to provide a clear width of thirty-two inches for wheelchair passage. Doorways should have no saddles so that chairs can roll through easily. It's difficult for a person in a wheelchair to back up, and both wheelchairs and walkers require a turning radius of sixty inches. Allow for this, especially at a doorway, where the person in a chair or walker must enter, then turn around to close the door. Keep this turn-around area clear. For wheelchairs and walkers, eliminate doors whenever possible. They're troublesome to open, pass through, and then close. When doors must be used, consider pocket doors that slide back inside the wall. If doors must be hinged, fit them with lever handles.

Inside the Accessible Bath

Vanity. The universal bathroom should have an open-base vanity counter. This plan allows anyone to be seated at the vanity. A wheelchair can easily roll underneath. Counter height will depend on individual or family preference. A woman might choose a thirty-inch-high counter. A six-foot man might prefer a thirty-six- to-thirty-nine-inch-high vanity top. The point is, fit the vanity height to the user's needs. Pipes for the lavatory can be hidden by a retractable tambour or some other type of panel.

A countertop-to-ceiling mirror will eliminate the need to maneuver to use the mirror. Retractable shaving mirrors can be moved close to a wheelchair. The magnifying side is useful for nearsighted and farsighted individuals.

Shower. Ride-in showers are recommended as the most convenient bathing arrangement for wheelchair users. A basic design consideration is to eliminate saddles or other threshold obstructions so that the wheelchair can roll inside easily. Build your own or install a preformed shower. Some manufacturers make a barrier-free shower designed to fit an existing standard-sized (thirty inches deep by sixty inches wide) tub area for easy retrofit.

Grab bars are recommended for convenience and safety inside the tub/shower areas. Place faucets near the outside of a shower or tub so that water can be turned on from there and temperature adjusted before the user enters the water. Install interior and exterior drains in the bathroom floor to take care of spills and splashes. Fit a shower with a seat if there is no roll-in shower chair. Whether you choose a bench or table for the shower, securely fasten grab bars to help the wheelchair-user swing from chair to seat. Hand-held showers, pull-out sprays, and body sprays installed at a height compatible with the chair, bench, or table are easy to use.

Toilet. The toilet should be a comfortable eighteen inches high for easy transfer from a wheelchair. Leave thirty inches of clear walkway in front. In order to leave enough space beside the toilet for a wheelchair, place the toilet on a straight wall and not in a niche. This also permits installation of grab bars, which are helpful to the weak as well as to those in walkers and wheelchairs. On the wall behind the toilet, securely attach grab bars. Choose the type of grab bar that swings up and out of the way. Provide one for each side of the toilet.

For additional information, please see chapter seventeen for sources of Americans with Disabilities Act (ADA) literature and organizations.

CHAPTER 13

The Home Office

The home office is relatively uncharted territory. There are no rules (yet) and few guidelines that apply, so creating our own home office means making a lot of purely personal decisions. So much the better. We can set our own office policies about furniture, art (where, what kind, and how many pictures we can hang), paint colors, and a host of other politically potent matters that often divide the corporate office. In short, whether we're I-G (income-generating) or C-A (corporate-affiliate) home office workers, we're free at last to create the ideal working environment with all the comforts of home. Where do we start?

Location, Location, Location

For some thirty-three million of us, working at home is akin to living above the store. A major challenge is to both separate and integrate our work and home lives. Success depends largely on where we locate the office. Don't fall into the trap of commandeering just any available space. You may discover that noise, traffic, and a million other distractions make conducting any kind of business there impossible. On the other hand, you may discover that the spot you've picked is too far off the beaten path. You feel lonely, isolated, cut off from civilization. The best time to take you, your office, and your special needs seriously is right from the start. You'll be far more productive if you're happy in your office.

The key to choosing the location that's best for you is knowing how you work best. Do you like to be near but not part of the action? Clearly, the basement won't do for you. Ideally, your office should be near the center of the home. We helped a friend convert a bedroom just down a short hallway from the living room in her Chicago high-rise into an office for her executive placement business. We replaced the solid wood door with a French door. True, the glass door let in more light, but the real reason we changed doors was so that she could see but not hear living room activities. The cheerful living room replaced a dismal view of the high-rise just outside her office window (which we closed with stock wooden shutters).

When the husband of another friend who works at home was transferred recently, they bought a tenth-floor condominium on a Florida beach. Before moving in, she showed her daughter where she planned to have her office. "It's a porch!" her daughter said in dismay. In fact, it's a glass-enclosed room with an exterior iron railing. Tinted glass walls are actually sliding glass doors with removable screens and floor-to-ceiling thin-slat blinds. The porch office is climate controlled. Views of the heavily trafficked Atlantic Ocean are on one side and Florida's picturesque Intercoastal Waterway on the other. They're a constant delight to this woman, who for the five years before worked in a Northeastern basement. "I did appreciate the bomb shelter quiet of my basement office," she says, "but the Florida sunshine, gorgeous cloud formations, and ever-changing views suit me much better. And, on the tenth floor, I enjoy the same kind of quiet without the sense of isolation."

A porch with a view may not be your cup of tea. Perhaps your office should be near where your small children are sleeping, or perhaps you're a chef, caterer, or cookbook author and need to be near the kitchen. If you're an architect in a big city, having a professional-level office in your apartment, brownstone, or loft is de rigueur. We know an insurance salesman who combines his home office and exercise room. An editor in New York City built in a long desk/work top across one end of a generous-sized dining room. On the wall behind, she built floor-to-ceiling bookshelves and cabinets to store her many stacks of papers neatly out of sight. A handsome, round, antique dining table serves as a conference table. Glass sliding doors look out onto one of the city's most pleasant sights, a small, beautifully planted garden. In the summer, it offers up a rare treat—conferencing al fresco.

The configuration of your office has to suit only you. A Pullman-like corridor, closed to through traffic, may serve the purpose. A corner of the kitchen might do. A certified kitchen planner in New Providence, New Jersey, showed us sketches for a six-feet back porch adjacent to a kitchen that he was converting into a home office. Two walls featured fifteen-inch-deep wraparound bookshelves beneath casement windows that looked out into a pretty patio. On the third wall was a built-in desk for a computer, with shelves above it that went to the ceiling. A pocket glass door closed off the tiny but terrific office without depriving the kitchen of the view of the patio (accessible through another exterior door). Perhaps you've seen similar or completely different situations that inspire you to seek your own special place.

How Much Space?

A recent major magazine showed the home office of an architect who houses CAD systems, laser printers, fax machines, telephones, and more in his twelve- by fourteen-foot space. In the same article, a nine- by eighteen-foot corridor houses floor-to-ceiling bookshelves on one wall and a countertop desk for telephone and electronic equipment and storage on the other. These and the other home offices we've mentioned differ radically in every way. They show that it's possible to have a home office, no matter what your space limitations are.

Start your space planning by listing the equipment you'll need: computer, copy machine, fax, and so forth. The nature of your work and the way in which you do it will influence the kind, quantity, and arrangement of furniture in your home office. This, too, will help determine how much or how little space you'll require. For example, if you do copious research, you'll need a lot of work surface for books and papers. A medical doctor who converted his dining room into a home office used his desk, credenza, bookshelves, and the floor for stacks of professional journals he was continually reading. His sympathetic wife kept the door closed at all times.

Which Desk's for You?

L-shaped desks, once considered secretarial, are replacing the old-fashioned executive desk and credenza. Executives are discovering what secretaries have known for a long time. It's easier and more efficient to turn from work surface to computer than from desk to credenza. Allow a five-feet-square floor space for this arrangement, or more if you augment the arrangement with a credenza behind the desk.

Writers and others who work with mountains of paper, two or more telephones, a fax, and a computer find a U-shaped configuration more efficient. They're easily and inexpensively created by placing flush hol-

low-core doors about the same size as a standard executive desk (thirty inches or thirty-six inches wide by seventy-two inches long) atop two-drawer file cabinets. Be sure to leave enough space between the right and left sides of your U-shaped desk so that you can maneuver easily.

Whenever you draw in a desk on your floor plan, add a minimum of two feet for your office chair, plus another two feet in which to push back your chair when you rise.

Custom-built furniture may be more expensive, but it often makes the most efficient use of space. If space is tight, you may be able to build in an adequate desktop that's less than the standard thirty-two inches wide, or you could build a desk with a space-saving breakfront (wider in the middle and narrower on the sides) or banjo (wider on one side, much narrower on the other) shape. Some rooms have oddly shaped nooks and crannies that require custom furniture to satisfactorily use the space.

A P-top (a desk that flares out into a wider semicircle at one end) saves space and is fast becoming a favorite in smaller offices that need both a desk and conference table. Popular-sized work surfaces are thirty-two-inch-wide work tops that flare to forty-two-inch-wide conference table ends, and thirty-six-inch-wide work tops that flare to forty-eight inches. Either can be attached to a matching standard six-feet-long wall unit consisting of a credenza with a file-drawer pedestal and optional bookcase hutch. They're available in all price ranges and come in a wide variety of materials, including fancy wood veneers and easily cleaned laminates.

Instead of using a desk, a space-saving ploy is to use a table that serves as a conference table as well as a work surface. A designer friend whose office measures only ten feet by ten feet bought a $250 glass-topped dinette table with a chrome base to use as her desk/conference table. Behind that, she placed a row of five black, metal, two-drawer file cabinets; each cost under $30. The 24-inch-deep cabinets served as desk drawers, file cabinets, and an auxiliary work surface. Guests seated in two pull-up chairs were able to rest papers and elbows on the table during long nose-to-nose meetings.

This designer chose a thirty-six-inch by forty-eight-inch glass-topped table because it was big enough and the transparent glass top helped make the small office seem larger. Your table might be Swedish modern, Chippendale, antique pine, maple, plastic laminate, a slab of granite or

Illustration opposite:
The U-shaped desk is generally the most efficient configuration for the at-home executive.

marble on chrome legs, a painted picnic table, or a panel of plywood across sawhorse legs. The options are endless.

Don't overlook the notion that you may need more than one desk just for your own use. If you do more than one kind of task, desks in different types of situations may help you get the job done. For example, if you spend a lot of time conceptualizing, a view may help. When you switch to putting your thoughts onto paper, you may need an enclosed area that helps you focus.

Making Your Space Your Own

Once you've decided which room will serve as your home office, take a critical look. Are there plenty of windows? If not, add them before you set up shop. Consider casement windows (the kind that crank open and closed). They're easier to open than double-hung windows. If there's a view, don't block it. Build cabinets, shelves, or window-seat storage below and around windows.

For better interior light and views, don't forget French doors. You can also lighten an interior wall by installing a window. Leave it open if noise is not a problem. Close it with a fixed pane to keep noise out. Close the opening only with operable shutters if occasional privacy is needed.

Will you need auxiliary heat for late nights or early mornings when central heating is turned off in the rest of the house? Will you need a separate air-conditioning unit? Do you need additional electrical outlets? Address these questions for maximum comfort and convenience.

Furnishings

Once you have decided on the particular space, you will need to turn your attention to furnishings other than your desk. One of the most important will be your choice of a chair.

Our designer friend who chose the contemporary glass-topped table/desk paired it with a wooden Bank of England–style chair that she spray-painted fire engine red. "The comfortable shaped saddle seats prove why these old-fashioned chairs have been around for hundreds of years," she explains. A wooden chair may work for her because she uses the office only for meetings and paper shuffling. She does not use her computer at the desk. If you work at a computer and/or spend most of your workday in your chair, don't choose one for its dramatic impact. Joel Levy, who heads a New York City–based office furniture distributorship, recommends selecting a swivel chair with five legs and casters for stability and mobility. Choose a model that's infinitely adjustable; that is, it can be raised and lowered, tilted forward and backward to any point. The seat should be well padded but firm for comfortable support. Upholstery fabric should be either leather, a high-quality vinyl, or a tightly woven fabric that does not attract lint or dirt. It should be easily cleaned—don't we all drink coffee at our desks? The armrests should be open and not confining, and they should be adjustable. By all means, sit on the chair before you buy it.

Guest chairs can be anything you like, as long as they're comfortable. A rocking chair, at home in President Kennedy's office, is a natural. Wing chairs are everyone's favorites. Place one by your desk for a guest and the other beside a small table where you'll read.

Storage can be as versatile as you like—install built-in cabinetry (don't overlook kitchen cabinet sources), shelves inside existing closets, and freestanding shelving from office supply or furniture sources. Armoires, antique bookcases, and salvaged gym lockers also serve as creative storage alternatives. Actually, rarely used equipment and supplies may be better stored in a remote location, freeing up your office for things you use frequently.

Lighting

Don't rely on natural light to replace artificial lighting, even in the daytime. Pay attention to the direction of natural light coming into your office and place computers and other equipment out of the glare. You may need more, not less, artificial light to balance whole walls of windows. Otherwise, the interior of your room will look like a dark cave in contrast to the brilliant light outside. Your eyes are precious. Don't hesitate to ask for advice from a local lighting consultant. Be prepared to install a variety of light sources, including general overall illumination and specific task lights. If your room is large, you may want to use two or more controls for ceiling lights so that you can light only the side of the room where you're working. Make sure that task lights are flexible and adjustable so that you can change angles and heights as needed. Check out the new long-life and special-function fluorescents. For more information on lighting, see chapter five.

Going Hi Tech

Those of us who work at home know that with a telephone, fax, and computer with a modem, we're never isolated from the outside world. All we need to do is push a button and the world is right there with us. In fact, one of the easiest things to do today is log onto the Internet. You'll need two private telephone lines: one dedicated to voice, the other to data. This allows you to talk on the voice line and at the same time send or receive a fax, or use your modem to send electronic mail.

Communication is increasingly important and machines that combine more than one communications function are increasing every day. Instead of installing a phone with an answering machine, you might want to invest in a more versatile combination of fax, phone, answering machine, and copier. Cordless phones free you to move about while you talk, and cellular phones keep you in touch at all times. If experts have one word of advice to those who work at home, it's to invest in the very best equipment you can afford. Up-to-date, efficient equipment keeps you competitive.

Home Office Convenience Tips

- Use surge-protector extension cords.
- Install waist-high electrical racetrack outlets just above your desk.
- Keep a postal scale, rate information, and stamps handy.
- Set up an account with an overnight carrier that makes house calls, such as Federal Express or UPS.
- Establish an account with a print shop to which you can fax an order for emergency stationery or office supplies.
- Keep Office Depot or Reliable Home Office catalogs on your reference shelf.
- Subscribe to the new *Electronic Home* (Advanced Housing & Home Automation) catalog.

Attics and basements are usually left unfinished by builders in order to hold down initial costs. These bonus spaces are ripe for finishing at a bargain price. Although local building codes may vary, most allow for conversion of these spaces for living. Check first to see just what restrictions may apply, and consult with an architect and perhaps a structural engineer to make sure that the changes you wish to make are feasible.

Both attics and basements offer unique opportunities for expanding your home to gain a much desired family room, bedroom, home office, or hobby room. Each of these spaces requires special design or planning considerations. Once you've satisfied these comfort requirements, you're free to decorate in your own personal style.

Attics: *Comfort under the Eaves*

Finishing an attic is one of the most economical ways of gaining living space, but economy should not be your only motivation. When Millburn, New Jersey, architects Jon Katz and Ileana Martin-Novoa were asked by a client to update an early Victorian house on a hill in northeastern New Jersey, the first thing they noticed was a magnificent view of the skyline of New York City thirty miles away from a tiny attic window. They decided that this big, untapped space was the best possible location for a wonderful family room. They created a wide, gracious stairway and installed a huge window that revealed a million-dollar view of the city and the surrounding centuries-old woods. Your attic may not have such a fabulous view, but having the chance to watch, at eye level, even one maple tree turn from bright green to brilliant gold in the autumn may be reason enough to make your attic a snug vantage point.

The Useful Attic

A useful attic must have a ceiling height of at least seven and a half feet in 50 percent of finished floor space. If yours doesn't, there's more than one way to gain additional headroom. Dormers of all kinds help do the trick, and if the view's worth it, you can raise the roof.

At least one window must provide emergency egress. In most places, local building codes will insist on this. In addition, for more light and

CHAPTER 14

Attics and Basements: Creating Bonus Spaces

❧

a view of the sky, add skylights. The easiest and least problematic to install are those that fit neatly between the rafters. The latest trend is to use several in a row vertically and horizontally to expand the view and admit the most light. If you want ventilation and the chance to enjoy cooling summer breezes, choose roof windows (skylights that open and close).

Before you pick up a hammer or call a carpenter, you'll need to have a professional stop by to ascertain if the existing structure meets the load-bearing capacity stipulated by your local code and to evaluate whether the space has access to heating, plumbing, and electricity.

During the remodeling process is the time to add insulation to keep the room warm in winter and cooler in the summer. If you're not sure how much you need, check with your local building department. In Portland, Oregon, six-and-a-half-inch R-19 batts in the ceiling and knee wall help keep photographer Kristen Finnegan's attic home office toasty warm all winter long. In New Jersey, R-13 batts in both ceiling and knee walls work in an attic converted by builders Ed Koza, Sr., and Ed Koza, Jr. Paneling and wall coverings supplement interior warmth.

A door at the top or bottom of the attic stairs controls noise flow between floors. A thick carpet with a dense pad will absorb sounds and dull vibrations. If your attic is going to get a lot of wear, consider a commercial-grade carpet, and be sure to carpet the stairs. Commercial carpets, made for hotels, retail shops, and other public areas, come in colors and patterns as interesting as those created for strictly residential spaces. The denser pile helps these carpets stand up to heavy use.

Attics are often converted into rooms for children, perhaps because it's difficult to move conventional furniture up the stairway (we don't all have grand stairways to our attics). Consider your furniture when you're measuring for stairs. If your stairway is narrow, look to modular, folding, and even flexible furniture. Don't forget built-ins. A built-in banquette for seating can be more interesting than a typical sofa and you can tailor the size to the space. The banquette should be at least twenty-four inches wide for sitting and fifty-five inches long, the length of a normal love seat. In an attic bedroom with no headroom to spare, a stacked mattress and box spring don't necessarily require a frame. If the mattress and box spring are just a little too low for comfort, stack

two mattresses on the box spring. We've used the two-mattresses-and-a-box-spring idea very successfully in a bedroom that needed a high-bed look to add to the period feeling.

Attics are great places to tuck in an extra bathroom, and what house can't use an extra bath, even if it's only a powder room? Actually, you only need a moderate amount of square feet for a bath with a shower, sink, and toilet. Designer Tess Giuliani of Bergen County, New Jersey, tucked such a bathroom into a tiny attic space. She carefully placed the toilet near the low knee wall and a custom-design neo-angle shower near the center of the space where there was adequate headroom. Because there was not enough space for a door to swing, she added a space-saving sliding door.

The Home Office and More

Attics are popular places for home offices. They're off the beaten household path, so they tend to be the quietest rooms in the house. If you use a computer and don't have to lug endless pounds of paper (catalogs, books, magazines, files, and so forth) up and down the stairway, they're perfect getaways. Look to RTA (ready-to-assemble) furniture for the pieces you'll need. They're easy to transport and come in popular desktop shapes, including T-tops (long ells) and P-tops (ells with a built-in conference table at one end).

Basements: Upgrading Below Grade

Basements are either totally or partially below grade (the ground's surface). This elemental fact presents problems that must be addressed before the basement can be considered a comfortable and healthy place for living and working. Your first move should be to determine if the structure is stable enough to stand up to the renovation process.

The next step is to test the stairs. Typical basement stairs are designed for infrequent use, and they are too steep for comfortable and safe daily use. If this is the case, you will need to rebuild the stairs to meet the building code and your own satisfaction. These two standards are not always the same. For example, the building code may allow a nine-inch-wide tread. For some of us, this means turning our foot to the side in a way that is uncomfortable and unsafe. A ten- or twelve-inch-wide tread is far more comfortable and less likely to cause a fall. In most cases, codes require access to the outside, especially when basement space is converted for bedroom use. The metal Bilco door is not glamorous but serves as a highly functional access to the outside.

Next, determine if there is enough headroom. You will need a minimum of seven and a half feet. If your basement ceiling is too low, consider excavating to gain necessary space. When a couple in New York City wanted to make room for a kitchen and family room, they excavated to gain adequate ceiling height. By excavating beyond the foundation at an outside entrance, they also gained a small patio with a central drain to keep water away from the door. It was expensive, but the pleasant living space they gained made it worthwhile.

Is there enough floor space for the purpose you have in mind? Most basements have pipes galore, water heaters, furnaces, and other mechanical equipment. They not only take up a lot of space, but are inevitably in the wrong place. Measure to see that you have at least the minimum amount of floor space for the new use.

Moisture Proof

Controlling humidity is the key to using your basement as a bonus living and working space. Comfort and function depend on this, especially if you plan for a home office, where books and papers will be stored. Mold, mildew, and water damage can destroy crucial work materials and mold spores in the air can trigger allergies and respiratory problems.

First check for leaks. Look along the floor and basement walls for damp spots and water stains. Even if there is no actual evidence of water, look carefully for cracks in the foundation that may indicate further trouble. If there is no evidence of water problems, count yourself among the truly fortunate. If you find even one hairline crack, consult a builder or architect to make sure the crack represents no future problems and that the basement is habitable.

Condensation, which occurs when cool surfaces collect moisture from warm air, encourages the growth of mold and mildew and the resulting telltale odors. Books and papers absorb this unwelcome mois-

Minimum Room Sizes

Bedroom	10 ft. × 11 ft.
Family room	10 ft. × 12 ft.
Home office	8 ft. × 10 ft.
Media room	12 ft. × 14 ft.
Recreation room	12 ft. × 16 ft.
Standard bathroom	5 ft. × 9 ft.

ture. To cure the condition, insulate the walls and add a vapor barrier before applying finishing materials such as wallboard, planks, or wood paneling. Also provide a vapor barrier between the floor and floor covering. Your building contractor will advise you as to the best kind. It may also be a good idea to install an automatically controlled dehumidifier that drains away moisture.

Peace and Quiet

Sound that travels between the basement and the rooms above and noise from mechanical equipment such as furnaces, air conditioners, laundry appliances, and so on, disturb household peace. Augment normal insulation with special soundboard to prevent this, particularly if the basement is to be used as a bedroom, recreation room, media room, or the home office of someone who needs a quiet space or will be using the telephone. For exterior walls, Georgia-Pacific makes a rigid foam board designed for insulation that comes in a choice of sizes. Your home improvement supply center will stock this and an expert can help you select the right product with the right R-value (resistance to heat flow) for your home.

Fresh Air

Ventilation is a must for basements. Include a top quality exhaust fan that vents to the outside in plans for a basement bathroom, kitchen, or laundry. Make sure that your dryer also vents to the outside. Install operable windows with metal frames to avoid moisture problems. Double-glazed windows will dampen outside noise. Cover any window wells with a translucent covering that lets light in but keeps rainwater from pooling.

Plumb Perfect

If you are building a family room, bedroom, or home office in the basement, a bathroom will be necessary for comfort and convenience. If there are already fixtures in the basement, putting new ones in the same place will save money. The rule of thumb is that it costs about $300 to move a fixture from one spot to another. If you must move a fixture, remember that the closer you stay to existing lines, the more money you will save. If you are adding plumbing where none existed before, do not be surprised if the plumber tells you that a sewage ejector will be necessary for a new toilet. This is not unusual when the main waste line is higher than the toilet will be. The convenience factor of a handy bath and the extra value it adds to the home should easily offset the extra cost of the equipment.

Wired

Take the time during your design process to envision where you will need outlets. Cutting corners to save a few dollars usually cuts down on comfort. It is also a lot more expensive to call the electrician back after your basement renovation is finished. Ask your electrician about outlet options. The most useful outlets are what are called racetrack outlets, a series of several plugs on a strip, installed just above the desktop to allow for many pieces of office equipment to be plugged in or moved to some other place without crawling on the floor to unplug and replug. Imagine your room furnished in a variety of layouts and take note of where, in each scenario, you might need to plug in a lamp, pencil sharpener, television or other equipment. Install outlets accordingly.

Separate circuits are required for special office equipment, such as computers, printers, and vital communications devices, and your heavy household equipment, such as your washer and dryer. Equipment that draws a lot of electricity will need its own circuit to prevent overloads. Why sacrifice your year end report to the rinse cycle? Just as in the kitchen, make sure that turning on your dryer downstairs and microwave upstairs won't cause a power interruption.

For safety's sake, install ground fault circuit interrupters (GFCIs) that turn off the electricity instantly when there is a danger of shock. GFCIs are mandated by most building codes in bathrooms and kitchens, but older homes are not required to retrofit. If that is the case, have your electrician replace these outlets. A real house comfortable (and house safe) will use GFCIs in the kitchen, bath, and wherever water or moisture is present.

Flooring

Options include resilient flooring such as wood, ceramic tile, and carpeting. Carpeting is a good choice for practical and cost-cutting reasons. In contrast to wood or tile, which may require expensive floor leveling and in turn will reduce ceiling height, carpeting can be installed quickly and easily over irregular, dry concrete surfaces. Carpeting comes in a wide variety of price ranges and also offers the comforts of sound absorption and cozy softness underfoot. It is also easy to clean. Carpeting comes in a wide variety of decorative patterns, colors, and textures, making it a beautiful as well as a comfortable choice.

Ceilings

Low basement ceilings do not feel comfortable. You may be tempted to merely leave wires, pipes, and joists exposed and cover them with a coat of black or white paint. Resist this urge. Add insulation between the joists, then paint, if you like. Or, add insulation covered by a layer of plywood between the joists, then paint the ceiling and any exposed wires and pipes. Your ceiling will have a high-tech look. If you find this too unconventional and prefer a more traditional ceiling, insulate and then finish with more conventional wallboard, wood planks, or acoustical tiles. Some architects advise creating a raised area in the middle of the ceiling or, if that is impossible, simulating this design by dropping the perimeter of the ceiling. Surprisingly, this creates the sensation of a higher ceiling throughout the room.

For installing lighting, you'll need to follow some general guidelines, especially if the ceiling just meets the bare minimum requirements for height. Avoid chandeliers or pendant lights in rooms with seven-and-a-half-foot ceilings. They will make the ceiling appear even lower. Instead, use indirect cove lighting or wall-hung sconces for overall light. Fluorescent lights are the most efficient providers of ambient light and are the best choice if you are using the space for a home office. Additional accent and task lighting can be used for increased productivity. Accent lighting may come from halogen track lights to create special effects on walls or to light artwork. Lamps can provide task lighting.

Basement Building Terms

- **Ducts:** Large, sheet-metal pipes that carry heated or conditioned air from the furnace or air conditioner to vents in the house
- **Furring strips:** Lengths normally one inch by two inches of pine or fir usually attached to masonry walls and floors as a base for attaching wallboard and flooring
- **Joists:** Parallel boards that act as supports for flooring and ceilings
- **Vapor barrier:** Usually plastic sheeting attached to walls and floors to prevent migration of moisture in and out of living areas—some manufacturers make tar- or asphalt-impregnated paper on one side to act as a moisture barrier
- **Wallboard:** Thin, wide board made of layers of gypsum and paper used as a substitute for plaster walls; sometimes called gypsum or plaster board

Hot and Cold

Tapping into the existing HVAC (heat, ventilation, and air-conditioning) lines is the most convenient and least costly solution to heating and cooling your renovated basement. Do give some thought as to where you will want new ducts to go and not to go. You won't want hot and cold air blowing across you as you work on your computer or try to get a good night's rest in the new basement bedroom. If it is not possible to add new ducts, there are several options including portable heaters and air conditioners. New zero-clearance, direct-vent gas fireplaces vent like dryers and can be installed even in high density areas, including New York City. These fireplaces do not require expensive, hard-to-install chimneys and they come in a variety of traditional and contemporary mantle styles.

CHAPTER 15

Home Security: Entering the Safety Zone

How safe and secure is your home? Safety measures reduce risk of accidental injury and death. Homeowners are required by local ordinances to meet basic safety standards. Most communities demand smoke alarms, radon tests, and other safety evaluations when property changes hands. Security is intended to protect occupants and property from crime. While most communities do their level best to increase protection of your property and person, there are no guarantees. Beefing up your own safety and security prevents losses and gives you peace of mind while you are at home.

Some homes are vulnerable to crime. Increased defense measures are advised for people who work at home or spend long hours alone during the day. At night, we all feel more snug in our beds knowing that we have taken steps to protect the people we love.

Safety Checklist

How safe and secure is your home? Check the boxes that apply to your home.

Outside Safety

☐ Do all your windows have working locks?

☐ Do all your exterior doors and entries have dead-bolt locks?

☐ Do you have a way of knowing who is at the door before you open it?

☐ Can the keys to your house only be copied by one locksmith where you are registered?

☐ Is your entryway well lit?

☐ Is the garage area well lit?

☐ Do you have motion detector security lights positioned at the sides and rear of your house?

☐ Do you belong to your community safety and security program?

☐ Do you have automatic timers on indoor and outdoor lights?

☐ Do you have an alarm system?

☐ Do you have a panic button that summons police or fire department?

☐ Do you keep trees and shrubs well groomed to increase the visibility of your lawn?

Indoor Safety

☐ Do you have working smoke detectors?
☐ Do you have carbon monoxide detectors?
☐ Do you have fire extinguishers available on each floor of your home?
☐ Do you have an immobile safe for valuables?
☐ Is there a phone in every room?
☐ Do you have a list of telephone numbers of family doctors next to the phone?
☐ Do you have a list of family members who need to be contacted in an emergency?
☐ Do you have emergency exits planned in case of a fire?
☐ Do you conduct fire drills or other emergency procedures (such as tornado, hurricane, flood)?
☐ Have you taught your children how to respond to an emergency?
☐ Do you have operable flashlights available in every part of your house?

The more checks you have, the better. Some safety and security measures are easy and relatively inexpensive to implement. Installing security systems may call for a little more time, effort, and cost. You can install a security system yourself (and save money) or hire a professional service. Professional installers seldom do any more than you can do yourself, and the price is higher. Newer homes often come with hard-wired security systems in place. If your home has no system, consider one that will at least alert you when there is a disturbance.

Your systems should have multiple sensors, panic buttons, motion detectors, light control, and about four zones. A single-family home needs only four to six zones. Eight zones is more than enough. Zones allow for separate sensors to be armed and disarmed. Zone 1 might be all outside doors, Zone 2 might be all motion detectors, Zone 3 might be inside motion detectors. Zones will enable you to arm all exterior doors but disarm interior motion detectors while you are at home.

Professionally installed systems offer monitoring features that are not generally included in do-it-yourself systems. Systems that connect to a twenty-four-hour central monitoring station provide additional protection. In these cases, interruptions and disturbances of armed security systems will alert an operator, who in turn will contact you (you must give the correct password) and, if necessary, contact the police, fire station, or ambulance. Make sure the system you purchase offers a monitoring station option. Monitoring stations are independent businesses, and many deal only with professional security companies. The monitoring fee is approximately $10 to $20 per month.

Never use the stickers that come with the alarm, advises one security consultant. Buy generic stickers. Many criminals know the shortcomings of different systems. They will know how to get into your home without alerting you, your neighbors, or your monitoring system. Don't give out information about your security system. Divulging what kind of system you have can jeopardize your security.

Most communities charge a fee for answering false alarms. Check with your local police department for more information. They can also tell you specifically about the nature of crime in your town and recommend ways to combat it most effectively.

Do-It-Yourself (DIY) Security Systems

These work just as well as professionally installed equipment and cost considerably less. Home improvement centers, hardware stores, and electronic stores carry security equipment. Comparison shop and talk to as many salespeople as possible. Also, ask your friends about their systems. Before you actually go shopping, you will need to have a rough sketch of your home and yard. Take into consideration how easy or difficult the system will be for other members of your household—from children to elderly grandparents—to operate.

Hardwired Systems

There are two kinds of systems available: hardwired or wireless. Hardwired systems, which consist of wires built right into the electrical system of the house, are the most reliable. New houses feature the hard-wired type. It's possible to add a hardwired system to an existing house, but it's considerably easier to install the wireless type that runs by radio frequency. Make sure that any system you install meets Underwriter Laboratory (UL) standards. Check that your system features the options you need. These might include magnetic switches, window foil, and motion, smoke, and carbon monoxide detectors.

Wireless Systems

These are easy to install. By sending radio frequency waves (RF) from sensors to a control panel, the system will alert you to a break-in or disturbance. Wireless systems can be installed with a screwdriver and, of course, there are no wires to run behind walls. These systems are supervised, which means that the control panel regularly sends signals to its sensors to verify uninterrupted communication. If a sensor is broken, the battery low, or a protected door/window opened, the system will issue an alert.

Self-contained System

This systems looks like a VCR with a built-in siren, motion detectors, and sensors. It is convenient to use and portable, but it protects only a room-sized area. Self-contained systems are best for hotel rooms and apartments.

Video Intercom System

This is an eye and ear to the outside world. There are two types available: easy-to-install integrated units or the more flexible separate components.

Integrated units have a built-in four-inch screen, a fixed-position B/W camera, a two-way transmitter, and a door release button. These are most practical when there is only one accessible entry. A camera and receiver stationed at your front door lets you see and speak to whoever is at the door. Make sure that the door and camera are well-lit at night and shielded from glare by day. At least one lumen of light is needed for the camera to operate correctly.

Separate components offer flexibility and the means to add more cameras that can be mounted out of view for front gates, rear entry areas, garages, and pools. Monitors can range in size up to twenty inches. This type of system can be outfitted with cameras that pan and tilt and require almost no light (infrared diodes pick up the image).

Color systems are now available, but generally they are much more costly. Most homes will probably not require such a state-of-the-art setup. The cost-effective, easily installed video intercom usually fits the bill.

Outdoor Lights

These increase the safety and security of your property. Lighting also adds to the value of the home, increases the beauty of the landscaping, and allows for greater use of outdoor space for entertaining and family activities.

Essential safety and security lights should be located at each exterior door, the garage, at dark corners, and near plantings around the house. Passageways to the street or driveway should be illuminated for clear and continuous visibility. No one should ever be in the dark on the way to the car or to take out the garbage. Key lights should be in operation from dusk to dawn. Others may be hooked up to sensors to conserve energy.

Not every light must be a floodlight to be effective. Decorative lighting accomplishes many safety and security tasks while adding charm. A well-lighted front entrance facilitates safe passage from the street or driveway to the door. Lights help identify whoever is at your door. Wall lanterns at each side of the door are decorative and inviting. Under a porch or overhang, use a recessed, chain-hung, or close-to-ceiling fixture. At side or back doors, install sufficient light to illuminate any steps or changes in grade as well as the keyhole. To conserve energy, consider post and wall lanterns that use compact fluorescent or high-intensity discharge light sources such as mercury vapor or high-pressure sodium.

For the safety and security of family members using the garage at night, install a wall fixture on the face of the garage. Fixtures equipped with high-pressure sodium bulbs deliver more light per watt and last many times longer than incandescents. For more control over light usage, use a photosensitve device to turn fixtures on at dusk and off at dawn. Energy consumption will be minimized, and security will be maximized.

Illuminate the sides of the house that fall into shadow. Use motion-detector or heat-sensitive controls that will switch on the light only when the house is approached. This works to keep away raccoons and other pesky animals. Use an automatic timer to control a portion of your lights. Basic security lights should be kept on until dawn.

If you are prone to losing keys, keyless locks can be installed. A combination of numbers opens locks and combinations can be changed easily. A variety of dead-bolt keyless locks are available.

Being safe and sound is an element of comfortable living. Taking practical and relatively inexpensive steps increases your sense of security. For more information on other safety and security options, contact your local police and fire departments. Many police departments offer consultations on ways to reduce your risks of theft and property damage. Once you have a system set up, be sure to use it regularly.

The air we breathe indoors is of great concern to health experts. Indoor air quality, referred to by its acronym IAQ, is affected by dust, mites, pollen, mold spores, bacteria, viruses, smoke, and noxious airborne chemicals. Poor IAQ may have long-reaching effects on health. According to the Harvard School of Public Health, childhood asthma has increased 35 percent, and deaths from asthma for all age groups has doubled during the last decade.

Air quality conditions within the home, even more so than in the workplace, could be responsible for these disturbing statistics. The indoor climate has changed over the last decade. Tight, energy-efficient homes and shoddy, cost-cutting construction have contributed to an unhealthy atmosphere. In some cases, older homes with cracks that allow the passage of air are often safer than their caulked and weather-stripped counterparts. The exception is in regions in which there is a high mold spore count as uncontrolled air exchange can bring spore-laden outdoor air into the home.

Poor insulation in any home promotes the dangerous buildup of molds and mildew, and the invasion of cockroaches and dust mites. Furthermore, the advent of wall-to-wall carpeting as the flooring material of choice has brought with it the golden age of dust mites. Keeping surfaces clean helps reduce problems, but the most dramatic improvements come from controlling the air itself.

How does your home's IAQ rate? Use the following checklist as an easy tool to help evaluate the safety of the indoor air quality of your home. If you respond "yes" to ten or more of these questions, you need to take some steps to correct IAQ.

Indoor Air Quality Checklist

Outdoor Toxins
- ☐ Do you live in the radon belt (east coast of the U.S.)?
- ☐ Do you live near manufacturing plants?
- ☐ Do you live near electric high wires?
- ☐ Do you live in an airport landing zone?
- ☐ Do you live in an area that had manufacturing plants that are now closed?

CHAPTER 16

The Air You Breathe: Maintaining Comfortable Indoor Air Quality

☐ Do you live near a large body of water—an ocean or a lake—where the humidity is high?

Indoor Sources of Toxins

☐ Do you have gas appliances? Are they properly vented and maintained regularly?

☐ Do the flames of any gas-heated appliance appear yellow instead of blue?

☐ Do you use a microwave oven that has not been checked for leakage?

☐ Do any householders smoke?

☐ Do you have furry pets who live indoors?

☐ Do you have an attached garage with parked cars?

☐ Do any householders pursue any of these hobbies indoors: oil or acrylic painting, car repair, woodworking, jewelry making, pottery, or model building?

☐ Do you use pressurized aerosol containers?

☐ Do you have a basement? Is any part of the living area below ground?

   ☐ Is the home insulated with polyurethane, ureaformaldehyde, or asbestos?

☐ Are the heating vents rusted?

☐ Do you have house plants?

☐ Do you use pesticides or insecticide indoors?

☐ Do electric outlets emit too much eletromagnetic radiation?

How Strong Are the Toxins?

☐ Does your air-conditioned air smell moldy, musty, or unpleasant?

☐ Are there any unpleasant odors of mysterious origin?

☐ Do you see moisture and mold on any windows or other surfaces?

☐ Does the air smell stale?

☐ Do any householders have any of the following symptoms: chronic fatigue syndrome; itchy, watery eyes; nose or throat infections; dryness of the throat; frequent colds, sinus problems; headaches; dizziness; nausea?

☐ Is the house temperature too hot or cold?

☐ Does furniture get dusty quickly? Can you see dust in the air?

☐ Are there dust or dirt stains on walls, ceilings, furniture, or curtains from air-conditioning duct sweating?

☐ Has the home been weatherized recently?

Householders at Risk

☐ Are there children under four years of age?

☐ Are there householders over sixty years of age?

☐ Do you work at home?

☐ Is anyone confined to the house for more than twelve hours a day?

☐ Does anyone have asthma, bronchitis, allergies, heart problems, hypersensitivity, or pneumonitis?

Other Toxin Factors

☐ Are there drafts?

☐ Are some parts of the house humid?

☐ Is the air too dry during winter months?

☐ Is the temperature satisfactory and controllable?

☐ Is there inadequate exchange of fresh and used air?

IAQ and Children

Children are at a greater risk than adults. Their metabolism runs faster and they are more active, which means that they are more likely to breathe in larger quantities of hazardous air pollutants. A higher metabolism means they are more likely to absorb contaminants more efficiently. Children's immune systems are less developed, so they are more likely to be harmed by a contaminant than adults. Their nervous systems are still developing. A pollutant, therefore, is likely to have a more profound impact. Their smaller size means that even a small amount of toxic chemical will severely affect a child. A twenty-pound toddler could be felled by a toxin that would have little effect on an adult.

Toxic exposure interferes with development and could result in learning and behavioral problems and lingering illness. Damage can be temporary or permanent. Long-term exposure to pollutants could lead to the development of certain kinds of cancers.

The Environmental Protection Agency (EPA) rates poor IAQ as the most significant health threat to children and adults. Spore-laden outdoor air, water pollution, electromagnetic radiation, radon, airborne lead contamination, and carbon monoxide are a few of the hazards that can affect a family's health.

To safeguard your child's health, the EPA suggests testing your home for pollutants and toxins. Kits are available from home improvement and hardware stores. In some cases, you will need to call in a professional. Test play areas and bedrooms for electromagnetic radiation from electrical wiring and appliances. Test drinking water for lead and other toxins. Test for airborne radon and lead. Install carbon monoxide detectors.

How to Improve IAQ

Effective control of indoor air can be accomplished by first addressing the source of contamination and then by improving filtration and ventilation. By addressing these three factors, you'll ensure that your home is a healthy environment for you and your family.

Source control means cutting off the problem at its origins. Simply cleaning more frequently and more thoroughly helps. Vacuum frequently. A number of new vacuum cleaners and systems have improved technology for removing debris and pollutants. Some vacuums promise to make the air, as well as your carpet, cleaner. Don't forget to clean blinds of dust buildup. Clean from the ceiling down to the floors. Use appropriate disinfectants and mold inhibitors on a regular basis. Hospital disinfectant sprays are available for use in private homes. If you are repainting, add a mold inhibitor to the paint mix. Remember, it is what you do not see that causes the most problems. The following strategies for keeping indoor air cleaner are inexpensive and easy to facilitate:

- Enforce a no smoking policy.
- Use only nonaerosol sprays to reduce hydrocarbons.
- Clean or replace furnace return-air filters regularly.
- Keep air ducts and humidifier reservoirs clean.
- Wash bedding frequently in hot water (130+ degrees) to control dust mites.
- Use a vacuum cleaner that filters air as it cleans.
- Ask your veterinarian about how to control your pet's dander.

Toxic Fume Management

To get at indoor pollution from oil- and gas-burning appliances, have them inspected regularly. Oil-burning appliances should be checked yearly; gas burners should be checked every two years. Inspectors look for proper operating efficiency, including a sufficient supply of air for combustion and to prevent backdraft. Backdrafting will carry fumes, such as deadly carbon monoxide, straight into the air supply of your house. A carbon monoxide detector hardwired into the house is the most effective first warning system. They cost about $70.

Radon Awareness

Another potentially lethal pollutant is radon, a naturally occurring radioactive material that causes cancer. It is odorless and leaks through the soil into the basement and is then circulated throughout the home. Newer, tightly constructed homes are more likely to be at risk for accumulating dangerous levels of radon. Many states require a radon inspection at the time of the sale of a house. If your state does not require a radon inspection or you would simply like to be certain, you can test your home for as little as $25. Test-it-yourself kits are available at hardware or home supply stores.

The Environmental Protection Agency recommends taking corrective action if radon levels are higher than four picocuries per liter. In this case, you would be advised to fill cracks in the foundation and basement, seal incoming water and sewer pipes, cover drains that penetrate the basement floor, and seal exterior block walls with polyethylene film. For high levels of radon, a contractor can put in a subslab ventilation system to draw air out from the basement and behind low-grade walls.

Filtration

Filtration of indoor air reduces pollen, mold spores, dust, and dust mites. The highest quality filters will also remove bacteria and viruses, a big plus if any householder is of advanced age, has a suppressed immune system, or is a toddler.

Whole House Filtration

In houses with forced hot-air heat or central air-conditioning, a filtration system is already built in. An upgrade is feasible—all you need to do is pick the type of filter that will accomplish your IAQ goals. The *fiberglass filter* that came with your system costs about ninety-nine cents and is rated by the American Society of Heating, Refrigeration and Air Conditioning Engineers (ASHRAE) at about a 5 percent efficiency for filtering out particles down to 0.01 micron. In other words, it will filter out a giant dustball but makes little impact on keeping your air clean. You will need to upgrade to a better filter.

ASHRAE rates *electrostatic filters* at 20 percent efficiency. An electrostatic filter places an electric charge on air moving through it. As the air moves across the filter, an oppositely charged filter attracts impurities. Semipermanent filters can be cleaned regularly and replaced every five years. Electrostatic filters are for whole-house application. You can replace the old fiberglass filter in your heating, ventilation, and air-conditioning (HVAC) system at a reasonable cost, about $40 to $70. Some have antimicrobial filters to prevent mold growth. They filter out pollen, mold spores, dust, and animal dander. To filter odor, get an electrostatic filter with an optional *carbon-impregnated foam filter* to soak up smells. Keep in mind that electrostatic filters may not remove bacteria and viruses.

A more efficient filter is a *media filter*, which costs $300 or more and must be professionally installed and replaced yearly. ASHRAE rates this type at between 35 to 88 percent effective. The better models have dense filtering material that is pleated to create more particle-trapping surface area. However, air pressure drops as it moves through the media filter. This may be a drawback because negative indoor air pressure causes backdrafting of fireplaces and gas- and oil-burning appliances.

The most effective whole-house air filtration system is the *electronic filter*, which uses electrostatic precipitation principles to trap particles so small you would need an electron microscope to see them. A prefiltration screen catches big particles, and smaller particles are passed through an ionization section where they become electrically charged and then trapped on metal collector plates. According to ASHRAE, this type of filter has an 80 to 95 percent efficiency rating. They cost about $1,000, are permanent, washable, and must be installed by a contractor.

Room by Room Filtration

If your home does not have a duct system, *individual room air cleaners* serve the purpose. Some recent models introduced on the market meet hospital clean-room standards. High-efficiency particle air (HEPA) filters, viewed as the best type of air filter, are made of deep-bedded fibrous material. They trap airborne particles regardless of size. Allergy-causing pollen, mold spores, smoke, dust mite debris, bacteria, and viruses are filtered out. Only one room per system is served.

Room filtration units are categorized by how much purified air they deliver. The Clean Air Delivery Rate (CADR) is a standard rating certified by the American Association of Home Appliance Manufacturers (AAHAM).

Ventilation

Beyond getting at the source of indoor air pollutants and maximizing a filtration system's efficiency, IAQ experts believe that ventilation is the single most important measure for maintaining good air quality. The best ventilation systems use continuously operating, low-speed fans that replace stale air with fresh air from outdoors. There are three basic types of ventilation systems: exhaust only, balanced, and balanced with energy recovery.

Exhaust-only ventilation comes in a point-of-source intermittent ventilation (think of the bathroom fan or kitchen hood) or whole-house exhaust. Point-of-source fans are a good starting point—they remove contaminated air, but they can't do much to clean indoor air. Most depend on being manually turned on and off. Newer models, designed to prevent mold from growing in the bath, have built-in humidity and motion sensors.

Whole-house fans remove air with a low-speed fan that minimizes drafts and noise. Vents placed in strategic areas allow fresh air in to replace used air, but the systems usually do not control air flow. One potential danger is the possibility of creating negative indoor air pressure, which causes backdrafting (described on page 197, "Toxic Fume Management").

Balanced ventilation systems offer a bit more control but use a single fan to expel stale air and allow in fresh air. The unit may be part of a central air system or ducted to key rooms. Balanced air systems introduce fresh air at a low point in a return-air duct. At that point, the fresh air is filtered, heated, and moved through the system and back into the rooms. In central air systems, fresh air comes in at one point in the house and stale air is removed at another. This can create temperature differences throughout the house.

That's where *energy recovery* comes in. In energy recovery ventilation (ERV) systems, fresh air is preheated with the warmth of outgoing air. A metal or paper heating exchange allows for the transmission of heat without mixing the air supplies. In cold weather, this reduces a draft situation and in warm weather, incoming air can be cooled. An ERV unit costs more than a balanced unit, but you'll see significant savings in energy bills and, more importantly, air quality and comfort are increased. ERV systems also help to control excessive humidity in the summer. In the winter, however, they may actually make dry air a little dryer, so you will need a humidifier.

Temperature and humidity factor in to overall air quality. Overly humid air can provide breeding grounds for molds. On the other hand, too little humidity is tough on lungs and skin. Relative humidity levels should range between 35 and 40 percent. To measure indoor humidity, buy a hygrometer at a home center. If relative humidity is below 30 percent, install a humidifier. Add a humidifier to the central system or use individual humidifiers.

Carbon Monoxide

Carbon monoxide (CO) is a deadly, ordorless and colorless gas that is thrown off by appliances that run on gas or oil combustion. Low-level CO poisoning mimics the flu with headaches, nausea, diarrhea, dizziness, and fatigue. Prolonged exposure leads to brain damage or death. Carbon monoxide poisoning kills about 1,500 people every year and sends another 10,000 to the hospital for medical treatment.

The culprits are inadequate ventilation, cracked furnace heat exchangers, and interior air pressure changes that create backdraft. Attached garages also cause problems, particularly during cold months when drivers let cars warm up in a closed garage while they sip a cup of coffee.

Carbon monoxide detectors can prevent accidents. They can be hardwired into your security systems, or you can purchase battery-powered detectors that can be plugged in or mounted on the ceiling. When the amount of CO builds up to a dangerous level, an alarm goes off. Some systems include a microprocessor that resets itself and a strobe light and automatic garage door opener that kick in when CO is detected.

Lead

Airborne lead poisoning is still a hazard. Although recent laws have eliminated and reduced lead in interior and exterior paint, some oil-based paints may still contain lead. Older homes may have higher levels of lead paint that can resurface when repair work or redecorating is in progress. The office of Housing and Urban Development (HUD) reports that 57 million houses still have lead paint.

Exposure to lead dust is the primary danger. New data from the Center for Disease Control (CDC) indicates that very small quantities of lead can be toxic and fatal. Be concerned even if lead levels are as low as ten to fifteen micrograms of lead per deciliter of blood. (Chemical analysis of blood is part of a routine physical examination. Ask your doctor or pediatrician for more information.) The dangerous level is twenty-five micrograms/deciliter of blood, down from sixty micrograms/deciliter in the 1960s.

Where does lead poisoning come from? Remodeling is one source. If your home was built before 1950, lead paint was most probably used for interior and exterior surfaces. Overzealous attempts to remove previous layers of lead paint by sanding and scraping mean releasing unacceptable amounts of lead into the air you and your family breathe. Most experts think simply painting over old paint is a far healthier solution. About three-quarters of houses built before 1980 have some lead paint, most likely on the exterior, says HUD.

Air-Conditioning

If you are adding air-conditioning (A/C) or upgrading, there are three basic categories to pick from, depending upon your house, needs, and budget: Room units, centralized A/C, and mini-split systems. All A/C systems consist of mechanical components that extract heat from indoor air and then transfer the heat outside. A compressor, condenser coil, evaporator coil, fan, and chemical refrigerant are the key components in this simple process. The compressor sends refrigerant to evaporator coils, which absorb heat from indoor air. The hot room air heats the refrigerant to a gaseous state. The refrigerant is then recycled and releases heat outdoors through the condenser coils. The refrigerant reliquefies and the cycle repeats.

Room units can cool one to two rooms. The cooling load estimate for every 400 square foot of floor space (with an eight foot ceiling) requires 12,000 Btus (British thermal units), according to the Association of Home Appliance Manufacturers (AHAM). Also check the EER (energy efficiency ratio) of the room unit, which is calculated by dividing cooling capacity, measured in Btu, by the unit's power consumption in watts. The acceptable minimum EER is eight, the maximum EER is twelve. The higher the EER, the lower the unit's operating cost, but the higher its up-front costs. The price of a room unit increases 10 to 15 percent for every two-point increase in EER.

Room units vary from 5,000 to 32,000 Btus and prices increase accordingly. To determine the real costs of the A/C unit, check the Energy Guide label that features the EER and operating costs. Comparison shop by looking at operating costs for similarly sized units at various EER ratings, then calculate the system cost to include energy cost differences.

Central Air-Conditioning

If you have to cool three or more rooms, consider central A/C. The compressor is located outside the house, the evaporator and blower inside. Cooled air is distributed through ducts. If you have forced air already, you can use the existing ducts. For putting in ductwork, consult an HVAC professional.

Mini-Split System

Mini-Splits feature separate handlers for air in each room and three-inch ducts. They are good alternatives if your present situation won't allow for extensive ductwork. Some homes, for example, would lose too much ceiling height if a central HVAC system were installed.

With any type of A/C, you will need to choose the best possible filter available and maintain the filters and ductwork, if any. Some maintenance can be done yourself, but central HVAC systems may require a professional with special heavy-duty equipment to come in to hygienically clean ducts. Mold and mildew can grow in ducts, causing allergy, asthma, and sinus problems.

Maintaining the quality of air inside your home means better health and comfort. Clean, conditioned, breathable air is not a luxury; it is a necessity. By reducing indoor air pollutants, controlling temperature, and regulating humidity, you increase your immediate comfort and decrease the risk of serious complications to your health.

The ultimate comfortable shopping experience involves shopping from your own home. The ease of mail order and Internet shopping have made the design and decoration process much more efficient. If you are crunched for time, can't get a sitter, or can't fit a trip to the mall into your busy schedule, then shopping by mail or at the cybermall is for you. Also included here are resources for Americans with Disabilities Act (ADA) information and products for those with disabilities and infirmities. The retailers and manufacturers listed here are known for their quality, value, and service.

CHAPTER 17

Resources: Mail Order Catalogs and ADA Sources

Mail Order

Art and Accessories

Exposures: A Whole New Way to Look at Pictures, 1 Memory Lane, P.O. Box 3615, Oshkosh, WI 54903-3615; 800/222-4947. Frames; curio cabinets; picture rails; file storage; picture lights, photo albums; vitrines; display ledges, decorative picture hanging hardware.

Sugar Hill, P.O. Box 1300, Columbus, OH 31902-1300; 800/344-6125. Hand-painted chests, tables; sofas, chairs; decorative drawer pulls; beds; whimsically painted furniture.

Ballard Designs: Accents for the Home and Garden, 1670 DeFoor Ave. NW, Atlanta, GA 30318-7528; 404/351-5099. Light fixtures; tables; mirrors; window treatment accessories.

Bed/Bath Furnishings, Textiles

Ballard Designs: Accents for the Home and Garden, 1670 DeFoor Ave. NW, Atlanta, GA 30318-7528; 404/351-5099. Four poster beds, other beds.

Chambers: Furnishings for the Bed and Bath, Mail Order Department, P.O. Box 7841, San Francisco, CA 94120-7843; 800/334-9790. Armoires for linen storage; furnishings for master bath; bath accessories; linens; towels; hotel and spa accessories.

Cuddledown of Maine, 312 Canco Road, Portland, ME 04103; 800/323-6593.

Egyptian cotton linens; towels; down-filled comforters; pillows; handmade pillows for bed in hard to find sizes.

Garnet Hill, P.O. Box 262, Franconia, NH 03580-0262; 800/622-6216. Handmade bed frames (authentic reproductions of American classic, contemporary), bed linens, pillows; European-constructed mattresses; mattress covers.

Lifestyle Fascination, 1935 Swarthmore Avenue, Lakewood, NJ 08701-4541; 800/669-0987. Mattress waterbed flotation pads, Real-Ease neck support.

Ralph Lauren: Country—The Home Catalog, P.O. Box 1100, Forrester Center, WV 25438-1100; 800/700-7656. Ralph Lauren furniture (chairs, beds, chests), bed linens, table settings, accessories.

The Company Store, 500 Company Store Road, La Crosse, WI 540601-4477; 800/990-8799. Down comforters, pillows; Egyptian cotton towels; blankets; bed linens; Ralph Lauren bedding; featherbeds (placed over mattress).

Schweitzer Linen: Fine Linen for Bed, Bath, and Table, 457 Columbus Avenue, New York, NY 10024; 800/554-6367. Linens, sheets; blankets; dust ruffles; duvets; down comforters; mattress padding; tapestry, needlepoint accessories.

E. Braum and Company, 717 Madison Avenue, New York, NY 10021-8090; 800/372-7286; fax: 212/832-5640. High quality luxury linens; custom-made special sizes; cashmere blankets.

Domestications: The Catalog That Brings Style Home, P.O. Box 40, Hanover, PA 17333. Linens; window treatments; bedding.

Bloomingdale's by Mail—At Home, 475 Knotter Drive, Cheshire, CT 06410-1130; 800/777-0000; fax: 203/271-5321. Beds; linens; blankets; pillows (also unusual sizes, shapes); furnishings; accessories.

Alsto's Handy Helpers: Practical Products for Your Home, Yard and Garden, P.O. Box 1267, Galesburg, IL 61401; 800/447-0048; fax: 800/522-5786. Motor massage mat; massage mat for office chairs; Aquapad mattress pad; massaging pillow.

The Sharper Image Spa Catalog, 650 Davis Street, San Francisco, CA 94111; 800/344-4444.

Dining In/Dining Out

Brookstone, 17 Riverside Street, Nashua, NH 03062; 800/351-7222. Outdoor dining furniture, cooking equipment.

Frontgate: Enhancing Your Life at Home, 800 Henkle Drive, Lebanon, OH 45036-8894; 800/626-6488. Professional outdoor grill equipment; outdoor kitchen island; outdoor dining furniture; accessories for bed, bath, outdoor, and car.

Crate & Barrel, P.O. Box 9059, Wheeling, IL 60090-9059; 800/323-5461. Outdoor dining furniture; rocking chairs; accessories.

International Wine Accessories, 111020 Audelia Road, Suite B-113, Dallas, TX 75243; 800/527-4072; fax: 214/349-8712. Climate-controlled wine storage cabinets, cellars; wine racks, racking systems; DIY cellar conversion kits; glassware; serving accessories.

Preferred Living: A Catalog from Sporty's, Clermont County Airport, Batavia, OH 45103-9747; 800/543-8633. Patio canopy; portable outdoor fireplace; patio umbrella; outdoor cooking equipment.

The Wine Enthusiast: Wine Cellars and Unique Gifts, P.O. Box 39, Pleasantville, NY 10570; 800/356-8466; fax: 800/833-8466. Wine-glasses, serving, wine cellars. Climate-controlled wine storage cabinets, cellars; wine racks, racking systems.

Stumps: America's Party Store at Your Door, One Party Place, P.O. Box 305, South Whitley, IN 46787-03045; 800/22-PARTY. Decorations, paper products for entertaining.

Oriental Trading Company, P.O. Box 3407, Omaha, NE 68103-0407; 800/228-2269. Decorations, paper products for entertaining.

Gardeners Eden, P.O. Box 7307, San Francisco, CA 94120-7307; 800/822-9600; fax: 415/421-5153. Outdoor dining furniture; furniture covers; serving supplies; decorative accessories.

Smith and Hawkin: The Sourcebook for Gardeners, 2 Arbor Lane, P.O. Box 6900, Florence, KY 41022-6900; 800/776-3336. Outdoor furniture for dining, in teak, metal; accessories.

Plow and Hearth: Products for Country Living, P.O. Box 5000, Madison, VA 22727-1500; 800/627-1712; fax: 800/843-2509. Rough-hewn dining tables, chairs; rustic accessories.

Schweitzer Linen: Fine Linen for Bed, Bath, and Table, 457 Columbus Avenue, New York, NY 10024; 800/554-6367

Home Furnishings

Ballard Designs: Accents for the Home and Garden, 1670 DeFoor Ave. NW, Atlanta, GA 30318-7528; 404/351-5099. Sofas, chairs: slipcovers; tables.

The Bombay Company, P.O. Box 161009, Fort Worth, TX 76161-1009. Sofas; chairs; tables; beds; cabinets; decorative accessories.

Crate & Barrel, P.O. Box 9059, Wheeling, IL 60090-9059; 800/323-5461. Bed frames; nightstands; sofas, chairs, coffee tables; outdoor furniture; rugs; accessories.

IKEA Catalog Department, 185 Discovery Drive, Colmar, PA 18915. Smartly designed Swedish-made furnishings for living room, dining room, bedroom, home office; storage; accessories.

Neiman Marcus by Mail: At Home, P.O. Box 650589, Dallas, TX 75265-0589; 800/825-8000. High-style country, contemporary, and period style furnishings and accessories for home.

Pottery Barn—Mail Order Department, P.O. Box 7044, San Francisco, CA 94120-7044; 800/922-5507. Overstuffed sofas, chairs; bed frames; tables; cabinets, chests, drawers; accessories; table linens and wallpapers.

Sturbridge Yankee Workshop: Decorating Your Home Since 1953, 90 Blueberry Road, Portland, ME 04102; 800/343-1144. Rustic, country style chairs, tables, sofas; decorative accessories.

Yield House, Department BI1000, P.O. Box 2525, Conway, NH 03818-9985. Furnishings in Shaker, traditional, country styles, all made in Shaker County.

Levenger: Tools for Serious Readers, 420 Commerce Drive, Delray Beach, FL 33445-4696; 800/544-0880. Library and home office chairs, desks, lamps, book storage, and nifty solutions for reading in bed or armchair.

Home Decorator's Collection: Where Value and Selection Come Home, 2025 Concourse Drive, St. Louis, MO 63146-4178; 800/245-2217. Specialties: Lighting (Tiffany look, prairie style), TV mounting kits, slipcovers, rugs, chairs, cabinets, accessories.

Solutions: Products That Make Life Easier, P.O. Box 6878, Portland, OR 97228; 800/342-9988.

Sundance, 1909 South 4250 West, Salt Lake City, UT 84104; Internet http://cybermart.com/sundance; 800/422-2770. Mission and golden oak furnishings for every room; Native American style furnishings; accessories.

Home Improvement
GE Plastics, One Plastics Avenue, Pittsfield, MA 02101; 800/451-3147. Lexan.

Improvements: Quick and Clever Problem Solvers, 4944 Commerce Parkway, Cleveland OH 44128; 800/642-2112; fax: 216/591-9490. Home repair and improvement for indoor/outdoor; flexible shower arms; wireless security; safes; wood repair; concrete repair; light timers and controls.

Renovator's: Manufacturer and Supplier of Quality Items for Your Home, Miller Falls, MA 01349; 800/659-2211; fax: 603/447-1717; out of U.S.: 603/447-8500. Lighting; bathroom, kitchen fixtures/accessories; wall coverings; tin ceilings; cabinet hardware; carpets and stair runners.

Jil Industries, 21 Queen Street, Maiden, MA 02148; 800/876-2340

Home Office
Brookstone, 17 Riverside Street, Nashua, NH 03062; 800/351-7222. Massaging cushions; leather ergonomic recliners; Shiatsu massaging recliner.

Reliable Home Office: Superior Design and Function for Your Home Office Environment, P.O. Box 1501, Ottawa, IL 61350-9916; 800/869-6000. Efficient filing, storage, desks, chairs, lamps, electronics, back support, footrests, and equipment for home office.

Lifestyle Fascination, 1935 Swarthmore Avenue, Lakewood, NJ 08701-4541; 800/669-0987. Office massaging chair, air filters (HVAC), air purifiers.

Sugar Hill, P.O. Box 1300, Columbus, OH 31902-1300; 800/344-6125. Home office furniture (reproductions of American antiques).

Home Safety and Security
The Safety Zone: Useful Products for Every Generation, Hanover, PA 17333-0019; 800/999-3030. Radon test kit; lead test kit for paint,

tableware; wireless security; motion detectors; fire emergency equipment; chemical-free insect control; cleaning equipment for home, yard, car; HEPA portable air purifier.

Perfectly Safe: The Catalog for Parents Who Care, 7245 Whipple Avenue NW, North Canton, OH 44720; 800/837-KIDS; fax: 216/494-0265. Water lead testing kit; microwave radiation tests; antiscald protection for bathtub; pool alarm; smoke detectors; HEPA portable air purifiers; kitchen safety latches.

The Real Goods: Everything Under the Sun, 966 Mazzoni Street, Ukiah, CA 95482-3471; 800/762-7325; fax: 707/468-9486. Comprehensive home safety kit; magnetic pollution meter (microwave, electricity); lead detector swabs; water test for ninety-three pollutants; shower water dechlorinator; water filter; energy-efficient lightbulbs.

Home Supplies

The Vermont Country Store, P.O. Box 3000, Manchester Ctr., VT 05255-3000; 802/362-2400; fax: 802/365-4647. Towels, bedding, sofa bed bedding, kitchen supplies, and country store favorites.

Good Idea! Catalog—Beautiful, Intelligently Designed Products for Use in Every Home, P.O. Box 955, Vail, CO 81658; 800/538-6690. Motion-sensor night lights, HEPA air cleaners; cleaning appliances, kitchen basics.

Kitchen Equipment

Sur la Table: Fine Equipment for Domestic and Professional Kitchens, 84 Pine Street, Pike Place Farmer's Market, Seattle, WA 98101; 800/243-0852 or 206/682-7212; fax: 206/682-1026. Copper pots; electronic kitchen equipment; accessories and table linens.

Crate & Barrel, P.O. Box 9059, Wheeling, IL 60090-9059; 800/323-5461

Colonial Garden Kitchens: The Total Home Catalog, P.O. Box 66, Hanover, PA 17333-0066; 800/CGK-3399; fax: 800/757-9997. Folding tables, chairs; equipment.

The Wooden Spoon: Specialty Cookware by Mail, P.O. Box 931, Clinton, CT 96413-0931; 800/431-2207. Work centers.

Williams-Sonoma, P.O. Box 7456, San Francisco, CA 94200-7456; 800/541-2233; fax: 415/421-5153

Personal Comforts

Self Care: Products for Healthy Living, 5850 Shellmound Street, Suite 390, Exeryville, CA 94608-1901; 800/345-3371. Back care—pillows, mattresses, back supports; pain relief; rocking chairs; HEPA vacuum; foot comforts; exercise equipment; PC aides.

Crabtree & Evelyn—Mail Order Division, P.O. Box 158, Woodstock, CT 06281-0158; 800/CRABTREE (800/272-2873). Massagers, home fragrance, soothing cosmetics.

The Sharper Image Catalog and The Sharper Image Spa Catalog, 650 Davis Street, San Francisco, CA 94111; 800/344-4444. Comfort gel for seats; Shiatsu massage lounge chair; massaging footrest; rolling massage pad; massaging ergonomic cushion; anatomical mattress pads.

SuperLife: Amazing Tools to Enhance Your Life, 18368 Redmond Way, Redmond, WA 98052; 800/865-7575.

Storage

Hold Everything: A Resource for Organized Living, Mail Order Department, P.O. Box 7807, San Francisco, CA 94120-7807; 800/421-2264. Storage systems for closets, kitchen, home office, TV/media room.

Lee/Rowan, 633 Etzel Avenue, Dept. HM 1293, St. Louis, MO 63133; 800/325-6150

Window Coverings

Country Curtains, At The Red Lion Inn, Stockbridge, MA 01262; 800/456-0321. Insulated shades; window treatments; decorative hardware.

Rue de France: The Traditions of France, 78 Thames Street, Newport, RI 02840; 800/777-0998. Charming lace window treatments.

Americans with Disabilities Act (ADA) Sources

Comforts

Adaptability: Products for Quality Living, P.O. Box 515, Colchester, CT 06415-0515; 800/288-9941. Wheelchair accessories; bed step; bed assists; pillows for sleeping; personal care–bathroom, toilet; grab bars; bathtub chair; reaching grips; heat/massage for chair; lift cushions for chairs.

Whitco, Box 335, Sausalito, CA 94966; 415/332-3260. Dumbwaiters and other helpful items.

Literature and Organizations

Accessible Building Design (free booklet), Eastern Paralyzed Veterans Assn., 75-20 Astoria Blvd., Jackson Heights, NY 11370

Adaptable Housing ($3 booklet), Dept. of Housing and Urban Development, HUD User, P.O. Box 6091, Rockville, MD 20850

Americans with Disabilities Act Accessibility Guidelines for Buildings and Facilities (booklet 9ADAAG), Architectural Transportation Barriers Board, 1111 Eighteenth Street NW, Suite 501, Washington, DC 20036

American Lighting Association (ALA); 800/274-4484

Association of Home Appliance Manufacturers, 20 North Wacker Drive, Chicago, IL 60606

Barrier-Free Design Workbook: Kitchen Design, Syracuse University All-University Gerontology Center, Syracuse, New York.

The Bathroom: Criteria for Design (2nd ed.), Kira Alexander, New York: Viking Penguin, 375 Hudson, NY, NY 10014, 1976

The Complete Guide to Barrier-Free Housing ($14.95, plus $3 shipping), Betterway Books, F & W Publications, Inc., 1507 Dana Ave., Cincinatti, OH 42507; 800/289-0963

Designs for Independent Living Do-It-Yourself Modifications Manual for Individuals & Families with Special Needs ($8.00 plus $3 shipping), Independent Living, Inc., 7360 N. Damen, Chicago, IL 60645; 312/973-4776

Designs for Independent Living and *Tools for Independent Living*, Appliance

Information Service, Whirlpool Fulfillment, P.O. Box 85, St. Joseph, MI 49085

Whirlpool Consumer Assistance Center, 800/253-1301 (translators available via AT&T Language Line); or, 800/334-6889 (Telecommunication Device for the Deaf)

Directory of Accessible Building Products (free, plus $3 shipping; Visa or MasterCard), NAHB Research Center, 400 Prince George's Blvd., Upper Marlboro, MD 20772; 301/249-4000

Product Search Services, Institute for Technology Development, Advanced Living Systems Division, 428 North Lamar, Oxford, MS 38655. ($0.50 per supplier listed. Photocopies of literature, $2 per product. Minimum charge, $5, plus $2.50 postage. Allow 3 days. No telephone calls.)

Fixtures Source List

Eljer, 17120 Dallas Parkway, Evergreen Center, Dept. HM 993, Dallas, TX 75248; 214/407-277

Maytag Co., One Dependability Square, Dept. 993, Newton, IA 50208; 515/792-7000

Peerless Faucet Co., 55 E. 111th St., Dept. HM 993, Indianapolis, IN 46208; 317/848-7933

Pressalit, American Standard Inc., 1 Centennial Plaza, Dept. HM 993, Piscataway, NJ 08855-6820; 908/980-3000

Sentex, Inc., 4340 Fortune Place, Suite A, Dept. HM 993, West Melbourne, FL 32904; 407/952-1300

Swan Corp., One City Centre, Dept. HM 993, St. Louis, MO 63101; 314/231-8148

Whirlpool, Appliance Information Service, Whirlpool Corp., P.O. Box 405, Dept. HM 993, St. Joseph, MI 49085; 616/927-7200

KATHARINE KAYE McMILLAN is a former senior editor at *20/20* magazine and now heads McMillan Associates Public Relations, Inc. She has contributed articles on building, remodeling, home improvement, lifestyle and interior design to magazines and newspapers around the country.

PATRICIA HART McMILLAN has twenty years' experience in home furnishings as a decorating and remodeling editor, interior designer, and design teacher. She is currently Director of Office Planning and Interior Design for Alliance Entertainment Corporation and the president of McMillan Associates Interior Design. Her private clients have included fashion designer Oleg Cassini and Frederick Haviland of Haviland Limoges China.

Patricia and Katharine McMillan, mother and daughter, collaborate frequently on real-life decorating projects, books, and magazine articles.